Mrs Darley's Moon Mysteries

A Celebration of the Moon: Her Phases, Myth and Magick

Carole Carlton

Copyright © 2009, 2020, 2022 Carole Carlton

All rights reserved.

ISBN: 9798476371328

DEDICATION

To all who have stood beneath the Moon and dared to dream.

CONTENTS

Introduction – Moon Rise	9
1 Moon Facts	15
2 Moon Myth	26
3 Moon Phases	55
4 Moon Tides	82
5 Moon Harvest	120
6 Moon Magick	145
7 New Moon Magick	161
8 Waxing Moon Magick	176
9 Full Moon Magick	195
10 Waning Moon Magick	215
11 Dark Moon Magick	239
12 Moon Set	260

ACKNOWLEDGMENTS

The beautiful photograph on the front cover is courtesy of the talented photographer Nicky Cousins via Picfair.com

My thanks as always, go to my loved ones, both on this plane and the next, who have always surrounded me with love and encouragement.

My gratitude goes to the many teachers I have been fortunate enough to come into contact with throughout my life, especially the precious few who have, or did, become treasured friends.

My appreciation goes to all who have come to know and subsequently enjoyed the Mrs Darley series of books.

My love and thanks as always, go to my husband William, for his editing and design skills in bringing this revised and expanded edition of 'Mrs Darley's Moon Mysteries' into print.

Introduction

Moon Rise

Mrs Darley Tale: The Naming of the Moon

'There.' My eyes followed Mrs Darley's outstretched hand as we leaned over her half stable door, one cool October evening. 'You can just see Her, beginning to rise above the high peaks of Dartmoor.'

We stood in silence and watched, as the full golden orb made its ascent into the night sky.

'The Blood Moon,' said Mrs Darley, 'so-called because the Celts believed that the spirit of a person dwelt within their blood. As summer came to an end and the harsh times began, they would ask their gods to strengthen the blood of the tribe so that everyone might journey safely through the winter.'

'Do all Moons have different names?' I asked.

Mrs Darley nodded. 'Indeed they do, and with good reason. Long before the Sun was recognised as the celestial body around which the earth moved, mankind measured time by the phases of the Moon. Eventually, seasonal names were given to each one, such as the Storm Moon, the Seed Moon, the Harvest Moon and so on.'

'How lovely. Those names almost lend a sort of romanticism to time.'

'Yes, I suppose they do.' Mrs Darley pulled the half stable door closed, indicating that we should once again return to the welcoming warmth of her fireside.

'You see my dear, our ancestors possessed a certain lunar

wisdom that we are only just beginning to reclaim, and although you are coming to understand the meaning behind some of our ancient seasonal festivals, you cannot become a true follower of the mysteries unless you have an appreciation of the Moon and Her phases.'

'I'm intrigued.'

'And rightly so. The Moon is an endless source of mystery and fascination, especially for you as a woman.'

'But why is the Moon so important simply because I'm a woman?'

'Because my dear, both our emotions and our menstrual cycle mirror the Moon. They constantly wax and wane according to Her light. Every woman should take time to attune herself to our cyclic Moon, for it is She who brings beauty and lust, fertility and birth, wisdom and retreat, all of which are precious gifts of the Goddess, from one woman to another.'

Introducing Mrs Darley

These were wise words indeed, from the enchanting Mrs Darley, the lady whom I was fortunate enough to have as my next-door neighbour upon moving to Cornwall in 1991.

Mrs Darley was an elegant lady of a certain age, who was surrounded by a delightful group of friends and acquaintances, each of whom readily shared with me their own unique view of life, love and magick.

The wild and mysterious backdrop of Bodmin Moor provided the perfect setting against which to undertake my magickal journey, and after a year of beginning to understand the Neolithic and Celtic Pagan festivals, my wise sage considered it was time to broaden my horizons by asking me to lift my eyes to the heavens.

Thus began my journey of becoming acquainted with the

Lady of the Moon: Her moods, Her cyclic nature and Her occasional unpredictable behaviour, all indications, as I was about to discover, of a true woman.

This book is an eclectic mix of the folklore, legend, spirituality and science that has become associated with our sole, but enigmatic satellite, whilst each chapter is interspersed with poetry and thought-provoking tales involving the charismatic Mrs Darley.

I would therefore like to invite you to embark upon a magical journey that ebbs and flows in rhythm with the Moon, and to encounter the Divine beneath the beauty of a moonlit sky.

The Birthday Moon

The morning of my thirty-second birthday found me feeling very sorry for myself. Snowed in on a dismal February day with a frightful cold and little chance of the postman putting in an appearance, I was sitting huddled over the fire with a hot lemon drink when a knock came at the door.

Reluctantly leaving my chair, I could see Mrs Darley standing in the porch, holding a pretty wicker basket, whilst enthusiastically stamping the snow off her shoes.

'Happy birthday, dear,' she said, thrusting a card and a circular gift into my hands as I opened the door. 'How are you feeling?'

'Oh, a little better thanks,' I replied. 'I can't get up the lane to go to work though.'

'Good.'

I laughed, knowing full well that she considered the snow a blessing in disguise as she often chided me for spending so much time working.

Throwing her coat onto a nearby chair, she picked up her little basket and immediately made her way into the kitchen.

Moments later she returned with a tray, upon which sat two mugs of hot whiskey and some freshly baked cherry scones, generously smothered with a generous helping of clotted cream and homemade strawberry jam.

'Oh my goodness, now that is a birthday treat,' I smiled, 'I can feel my appetite returning already.'

'Well, you enjoy them my dear.' She turned and nodded towards my present. 'Aren't you going to open it?'

I set down my plate, along with my half-eaten scone and carefully began to peel away the gift-wrap. Beneath, I found a layer of bubble wrap, followed by several layers of blue tissue paper. Finally, I held in my hands the most beautiful circular wall mirror, upon which was painted a waxing and waning crescent Moon either side of a full orb.

'Oh, it's beautiful.' I was genuinely delighted with this unexpected gift. 'Thank you. I've never seen anything quite like it.'

'A friend of Phyllis' made it for me,' said Mrs Darley.

I smiled as I thought of Phyllis, the lady who was Mrs Darley's oldest and dearest friend and for whom I had a definite soft spot.

'Well, Phyllis's friend is a very talented lady,' I said, 'and you couldn't have bought me anything better, especially following our conversation regarding the importance of the Moon to women.'

'Absolutely my dear, for not only does the Moon, imitate a woman's monthly reproductive cycle, she also mirrors our life cycle as we journey from Maiden to Mother and from Mother to Crone.'

'That's fascinating. I've never looked at the Moon in that way before.'

'Well,' she said, 'whenever you look into this mirror in the future, you will be reminded of this natural progression and it will invite you to reflect on the sacred cycle of life.'

I felt tears of gratitude begin to blur my vision. It was turning out to be a most remarkable birthday. 'I don't know what to say,' I whispered.

'Nothing is often best my dear,' replied Mrs Darley, her hand closing gently over mine. 'Happy Birthday.'

The following poem was the first poem I wrote when embarking upon the Mrs Darley series of books. My husband and I were staying in Somerset for a few days, and as we drove back towards Wells, the full midsummer Moon was just rising into the evening sky. She was breathtakingly beautiful and became my inspiration for the *Keeper of Secrets*.

Keeper of Secrets

Lady of the Moon,
Keeper of secrets,
In many guises,
And through many lifetimes
Have I gazed upon your infinite beauty.

I lift my eyes to meet your face,
And see life reflected,
Through the timeless mirror
Of your cyclic dance.

Beneath you my features soften,
Beneath you my voice is but a whisper,
Beneath you I am enchanted,
Beneath you I awake.

Beneath you I am bewitched,
Beneath you I call my gods,
Beneath you I weave my magick,
Beneath you I am changed.

Beneath you my shadow speaks,
Beneath you desire burns,
Beneath you I covet wild delights,
Beneath you I find myself.

Chapter One

Moon Facts

Mrs Darley Tale: Moon Water

The gentle light of the waxing mn gibbous moon lit my path as I quietly closed the five barred gate and made what I soon realised, was a futile attempt to tip toe silently along the gravel path.

'Lovely night.'

'Oh.' I swung around and dropped my bag at the sound of Mrs Darley's voice. 'You made me jump. I didn't think anyone would still be up at this time of night, well not in their garden at any rate. It must be nearly 2am.'

Mrs Darley laughed, and approached her garden gate with what looked like a watering can in her hand.

'Were you watering your garden?' I couldn't help sounding surprised, for no one I knew watered their garden in the middle of the night.

'Yes my dear, I was. I was just coming back from seeing Phyllis up to her car on the lane, when I suddenly remembered I hadn't watered my ailing clematis.'

'Couldn't it have waited until morning?' I asked.

'Not if I wanted to give it some Moon water.'

'Moon water?'

'Yes dear - rainwater that has been exposed to the rays of the Moon.'

'And will that make a difference to your clematis as opposed to tap water?'

'But of course. Rainwater that has been exposed to the

energies of the Moon is full of gentle, healing power, which is just what an ailing plant needs, whereas tap water is harsh, dead and full of chemicals.'

'It's something I've never even considered,' I said. 'So what you're saying is that the Moon can actually affect the energy of water?'

'Well, if it can affect the tides, then why not this?' She asked, lifting her watering can.

'I see your point.'

'She *is* beautiful tonight though, isn't she?' Mrs Darley gazed up towards the night sky.

I too looked up at the Moon in all her full glory. 'She is indeed. Although I do sometimes wonder how She got there.'

'Well, that my dear, remains one of the mysteries of the universe.'

'What - no one actually knows? Not even in this day and age?'

Mrs Darley shook her head. 'Not for certain, no, although everyone has their own theory of course. Look, I know it's late – or early depending on your point of view, but I think I might just have a drop of something to keep us warm tucked away in the summer house, if you'd care to join me?'

Never one to pass up an invitation to talk to my charismatic next-door neighbour, regardless of the hour, I soon found myself ensconced in a faded, but comfortable old cane chair, next to the increasing warmth of an oil filled radiator that Mrs Darley had thoughtfully switched on as we entered.

'You know, I'm amazed,' I said, sipping my whiskey. 'I thought that in these modern times with all the backing of science and numerous Moon landings, that someone could surely answer the question of how the Moon came to be in our orbit.'

'Ah,' Mrs Darley leaned forward and tapped her nose with her finger. 'You forget my dear, that the Moon is a woman –and a woman *never* reveals all her secrets.'

Lunar History and Geology

The Moon is our only satellite, and as such, has been the object of discussion and debate since man first came into being. Questions have been asked and answers proffered as to how She came to be here, what She comprises of, why She behaves so strangely, and how She affects everything that lives upon the Earth.

The answers, like the questions, are many and varied, but let us begin by considering some of the theories suggested by the scientists.

Theory One: The Fission theory

Sir George Darwin, son of the famous naturalist, thought that the Earth and Moon were originally one body and that the Moon was, at some point, thrown off in a liquid mass and began to orbit the Earth, caught by its gravitational pull.

An American astronomer called W. H. Pickering, took this theory one step further and said that where the separation took place, a large hollow formed and was filled by the Pacific Ocean, whilst the force of the separation caused faults in the Earth's surface under the ocean bed.

However, mathematicians later discovered that these theories simply could not work as the Moon would have broken up due to the terrific force of the separation, and fallen back to Earth as debris.

Theory Two: The Capture Theory

The Moon was once believed to be an independent planet, orbiting the Sun between Earth and Mars, before venturing close enough to Earth to be captured by its gravitational pull.

Patrick Moore however, the famous astronomer, pointed out that this could only occur under exceptional circumstances, i.e. that the Moon slowed down by just the right amount and at just the right time to be captured, otherwise it would either hit the Earth full on, or would rush past it and remain as an independent planet.

Theory Three: The Condensation theory

In 1974, W. Hartmann and D. R. Davis, of the Planetary Science Institute, proposed that the Earth and the Moon were formed separately from the nebula (the initial cloud of gas and dust) that gave birth to the solar system.

If this theory is true, then Earth and Moon should have very similar compositions, including an iron core, but this is not the case. In addition, the Moon appears to have been 'baked' more than the Earth, and is believed to have formed at a much higher temperature, i.e. between 2,200 to 3,300 degrees Celsius.

Theory Four: The Giant Impactor Theory / The Theia Theory / The Ejected Ring Theory

Regardless of this fourth theory having several names, the idea was originally proposed back in 1969. It suggested that around 4.45 billion years ago, a small planet, the size of Mars, struck Earth shortly after the formation of the Solar System, generating energy 100 million times greater than the event which is believed to have wiped out the dinosaurs.

This rogue planet was eventually named Theia, after the Greek Titan of the same name, who gave birth to the Moon Goddess Selene. The name was chosen by the English geochemist, Alex N. Halliday in 2000CE and has since been accepted by the scientific community.

Theia was thought to have been destroyed on impact, but the heated material created from the outer layers of both planets was ejected into the Earth's orbit, and formed an orbiting disk that was then captured by the Earth and became our Moon. Although this theory answers many questions, it still leaves some moot points, which will no doubt continue to be debated by scientists in the years to come.

Understanding the Moon

Regardless of how the Moon came to orbit the Earth, it is thought that during its formation (some four billion years ago), it experienced a large amount of volcanic activity, but due to its small size, it cooled very quickly and became the satellite we are familiar with today.

The Moon is approximately 238,000 miles away from Earth (equivalent to ten times the distance around the Earth's circumference), and always shows the same face to the Earth. This is due to the constant gravitational pull of the Earth on the Moon, which has slowed down the Moon's rotation so much that it is now in synch with that of its orbit (approximately 27.3 days), a phenomenon that is referred to as 'tidal locking'. If the Moon rotated either faster or slower, we would be able to see its other half, or the 'dark side of the Moon' as it is often known.

When we refer to 'half' the Moon, we usually assume that this means fifty percent. It is however, possible to see up to fifty nine percent of the Moon's face during its monthly orbit, albeit not at any one time, and this is due to two factors:

- The Moon's orbit is elliptical rather than circular and is inclined towards the Earth at an angle of five percent.
- The Moon's speed varies according to its closeness to Earth.

These anomalies in the Moon's movement, often provides us with a glimpse of otherwise hidden areas, a phenomenon known as 'libration'.

The fact that the remaining forty one percent remains permanently out of view has, over time, caused some very imaginative theories to be put forward in order to explain what is there.

During the nineteenth century, the Danish astronomer Peter Andreas Hansen, believed that the Moon was actually lopsided and that all of its air and water had been drawn round to the far side. This led to many theories regarding the Moon being inhabited on its dark side.

In 1959 however, the Russians dispatched the spacecraft Luna 3, which went right around the Moon, and sent back pictures from the dark side for the first time, in an attempt to prove that life on the Moon did not exist. What the pictures did show however, is that the landscape on the dark side of the Moon is slightly different to the face we see from Earth, and does not appear to have any of the dark plains we refer to as seas.

The Moon consists of many curious, yet strangely beautiful features, the most well-known of which are the dark seas, originally named because they were once considered to be actual seas or, at the very least, dried seabeds. Moon samples from the lunar landings however, suggest that there has never been any water on the Moon, and that the 'seas' are simply smooth, dry lava plains, albeit the word 'sea' has remained in use.

Many of these seas are large enough to see with the naked eye, and have been given romantic names that stir the imagination, such as the Sea of Clouds, the Bay of Rainbows, and the Ocean of Storms.

The lunar surface is also littered with craters, the largest of which are some hundred miles in diameter. The crater Copernicus, situated on the north-eastern side of the Sea of Clouds, is fifty-six miles in diameter and rises in parts along its edge to heights of 12,000 feet. Generally, the craters are named after historical personalities including some Roman Emperors, such as Claudius and Caesar, although the majority carry the names of scientists such as Kepler, Ptolemy and Copernicus.

Other lunar features include the valleys, such as the less romantically named, 'Great Gash', that cuts through the 'Alps', on the edge of the "Sea of Rains', and other great mountain ranges such as the 'Apennines'.

The origins of these strange lunar features have become topics of debate over the years, and several theories have been put forward regarding their formation. These have included external impacts from collisions with other planets and/or asteroids, to claims that they were created internally by moonquakes and volcanic activity.

Mrs Darley Tale: Moon Wisdom

As we sat enjoying our second glass of the revered grain, the Moon had travelled across the sky and was now visible through the glass doors of the summer house.

'Quite simply my dear,' said Mrs Darley, 'we couldn't live

without the Moon.'

'Couldn't we?'

She smiled. 'I detect a note of scepticism in your voice.'

'Well, I suppose I'm wondering how a mere lump of rock that happens to be caught in Earth's orbit, could possibly affect us so dramatically.'

'Oh, my dear, that "mere lump of rock" as you so quaintly put it has many roles, ranging from those which can be historically or scientifically proven, to those that can only be imagined, or felt deep within the human psyche.'

Now I felt rather out of my depth. 'Such as?'

'Well, historically and archaeologically, She has been shown to be the sole timepiece of early man, whilst scientifically, She controls the tides and influences our weather patterns. There are also many gardeners who will only attend to certain horticultural duties if the Moon is in the correct phase or sits within a particular zodiacal sign.'

'Goodness me,' I laughed, 'I just do the garden if I've got time and it's not raining.'

'As do many,' said Mrs Darley, 'so you're certainly not alone, but those who do plant and reap according to the Moon say that the results are quite astonishing. I believe the head gardener at Tresillian House, the National Trust property near Newquay, follows Moon lore.'

'In that case, I will go and visit and see the results for myself. You mentioned the Moon affects us psychologically - in what way exactly?'

'Well, many believe She influences our moods and behaviour, and it is sometimes claimed there are more admissions to mental hospitals, or asylums as they were once known, at the full Moon. Hence the term, 'lunatic asylum', from Luna, Goddess of the Moon.'

'How fascinating,' I said, suddenly understanding the connection. 'I've never considered the actual root of that phrase before. So it was because people were adversely affected by the Moon?'

Mrs Darley nodded. 'Yes. In fact, over the years, the Moon has been held responsible for life, death and destruction.'

I listened in wonder to her words, wondering why I had never given either thought or credence to our beautiful night-time visitor before.

'Of course,' she added, 'the one constant, is that She has been, and still remains, a focus of worship and a powerful energy source in both magick, and ritual.'

I looked at her and smiled, unsure as to what she meant, and not confident enough to question, but she must have sensed what I was thinking.

'Our Lady Moon is the Awakener. She stirs the imagination and ensures that the consciousness of everyone who stands beneath Her is changed, a fact my dear, I hope you will soon discover for yourself.'

Moon Cycles and Behaviour

The Moon is an unusually large satellite in relation to the planet it orbits; only the dwarf planet Pluto's Moon, Charon, is larger. As a consequence, there is a strong gravitational attraction between the Moon and the Earth. In fact, the Moon's pull is two and a half times that of the Sun, and when the Moon moves closer to the Earth, this attraction increases.

The Earth revolves around the Sun once a year, whilst the Moon revolves around the Earth once every 27.323 days and is measured in relation to a fixed star. This period of time is known as a *sidereal* month, with the word, sidereal, being derived from the Latin, *sidus*, meaning star.

However, it takes 29.53 days for the Moon to pass

through all its phases from new Moon to new Moon, and this is known as a *synodic* month. This derives from the Greek word, *synodos,* meaning meeting, and refers to the meeting of the Sun and the Moon.

This discrepancy between the sidereal month and the synodic month is caused by the fact that the Earth itself is also moving, therefore the Moon must continue travelling for a further 2.207 days in order to once again realign itself with the Sun.

The phases of the Moon are caused by varying degrees of reflected sunlight falling upon the lunar surface. The smaller the angle between the Moon and the Sun, the less of the Moon is illuminated. When the angle is approximately six degrees, we see the waning or waxing crescent Moons.

On rare occasions, when the angle between the Sun and the Moon is exactly zero degrees, a total solar eclipse is experienced, resulting in a dramatic spectacle where the Sun's light grows dim and the temperature drops as the Moon passes between the Earth and the Sun.

Alternatively, when the angle between the Sun and the Moon is almost 180 degrees, we experience a full Moon. When the angle is exactly 180 degrees (an event that happens approximately twice a year), we are then able to see the Earth's shadow covering the Moon, and witness a lunar eclipse.

The Moon however, as Mrs Darley pointed out, is much more than just a piece of rock that happens to be trapped by the Earth's gravitational pull, for Her presence reaches deep into every nook and cranny of life here on Earth, as this book sets out to explore.

The seas, lakes, bays and marshes of the Moon have such beautiful names, that this poem was simply calling out to be written.

Luna

I am the nectar
That sweetens your dreams.
I am the cloud
That carries the rain.
I am the rainbow
That colours the storm.
I am the fear
That nurtures your sorrow.
I am hope,
I am serenity,
I am knowledge,
I am Luna.

Chapter Two

Moon Myth

Mrs Darley Tale: Inanna

I grabbed the torch from the shelf in the porch and switched it on before stepping out into the night. I was only going next door, but without the Moon to light my way, our little moorland hamlet was engulfed in thick darkness.

I had been invited to join Mrs Darley, Phyllis, and our neighbours from the cottage that faced out onto the lane, Bod, Rose, and their eleven-year-old daughter Lucy, for supper. It was Rose's forty-something birthday and I was late.

'Hello dear, come in, come in.' Mrs Darley opened the door and I entered her cottage with a bouquet of flowers for Rose and a bottle of claret as my contribution to the supper.

'I'm sorry I'm so late,' I said. 'I hope I haven't held up proceedings.'

'Not at all dear,' she replied. 'In fact, you're just in time. I was about to serve.'

With the six of us soon squashed cosily around Mrs Darley's dining table, the wonderful aroma of Indian spices filled the room as we helped ourselves and each other, to what was more of a feast than a supper. Poppadoms, naan breads, biriyanis and masalas each found their way to the table, all of which was accompanied by a deep, rich red wine.

'How's your ankle now, Rose?' Mrs Darley asked, helping Bod to the last of the rice.

'Not too bad, thank you.' Rose looked down briefly at her

foot.

'Why,' I asked, 'what have you done?'

'Oh, it's nothing really,' she said. 'We never thought to bring a torch with us when we walked round here earlier on, and as I came through the gate, I tripped over and twisted my ankle.'

'I'm sorry to hear that,' I said, 'and I know this probably sounds ridiculous, but I thought it was particularly dark tonight when I stepped outside.'

'Dark Moon,' said Mrs Darley.

I looked at her and frowned. 'What's that? I don't think I've heard the term.'

'It means that the Moon isn't visible in the sky. She's busy changing from her waning to waxing phase.'

'I've never really thought about the Moon changing from waning to waxing, and not being visible before,' I said.

Phyllis smiled. 'Then I take it you won't have heard Mrs D's story of Inanna?'

I shook my head.

'Oh, this is my very favourite story,' said Lucy, clapping her hands.

'And you,' said Phyllis, smiling at me, 'are in for a treat.'

Mrs Darley looked around at her guests. 'Very well. If everyone has finished, let us all leave the table, take a glass of whiskey, or orange juice for you Lucy dear, and settle ourselves beside the fire.'

Feeling replete, and with drinks in hand, we all gathered around the slumbering fire, whilst the flickering flames of the candles danced gracefully across the granite chimney breast.

'Way back in the mists of time,' Mrs Darley began, leaning back into her chair, 'in the land of Mesopotamia, there lived a Goddess called Inanna, daughter of the Moon. She was the eldest daughter of the Moon God Sin, and Ningal, the

Goddess of the marshes. Inanna had two siblings, Her brother Utu, the Sun God, and Her sister Ereshkigal, Goddess of the Underworld. She also had a lover, whom She loved above all others, a shepherd, called Dumuzi, the Lord of Life.'

'Sounds like me and you love,' laughed Rose, nudging her husband.

'Quite,' said Mrs Darley dryly. 'Anyway, one day, Inanna learned that Her brother-in-law, Ereshkigal's husband, had died, and so Inanna decided that She would travel to the Underworld of Kur to attend his funeral and offer Her condolences to Her pregnant sister, the dark Queen. And so...'

To my surprise, everyone suddenly stood up and began to recite a piece of prose, accompanied by a mime.

'From the great above,' they chorused, raising their hands into the air, 'Inanna opened Her ear to the Great Below.' They each cupped their hands around their ears before saying, 'and abandoned heaven and Earth to descend into the Underworld.' As they finished, they all pointed their fingers down towards the Earth.

'You'll have to join in next time,' said Phyllis smiling as they all sat down. Obviously I must have looked quite bewildered.

'Now, before Her journey,' continued Mrs Darley, 'Inanna had dressed Herself in the seven bright jewels of heaven for protection. These included a crown, lapis beads, double beads, a breastplate, a gold ring, a lapis measuring rod and line, and a royal robe. But despite these items of protection, Inanna still had concerns for Her own safety. She was, after all, going to visit the Queen of the Underworld. Inanna therefore asked Her faithful companion Ninshubur, if she would go to the house of the gods and express her sorrow, should her mistress fail, after three nights, to return to the

Great Above. And so...'

Once again everyone stood up, myself included. 'From the great above,' we said, raising our hands in the air, 'Inanna opened Her ear to the Great Below.' We cupped our hands around our ears, before pointing downwards to the Earth adding the words, 'and abandoned heaven and Earth to descend into the Underworld.'

'So,' continued Mrs Darley as we all sat down again, 'Inanna set off on Her journey and eventually arrived at the outer gates of the Underworld, whereupon She knocked loudly. The gatekeeper, Neti, called to Her and asked, "Who is there?" to which Inanna replied, "It is I, Inanna, Queen of Heaven, on my way to the East."

'Now, Neti immediately took this news to Ereshkigal, Queen of the Underworld, and Ereshkigal, who was jealous of her beautiful sister, instructed Neti to bolt the seven gates of the Underworld without delay. Ereshkigal then told Neti to open each gate one by one so that Inanna might enter, but that at each gate, Innana was to remove one of her royal garments.'

'And, one by one, Inanna was stripped of Her protective items, finally entering the throne room of Ereshkigal naked. Then...' Mrs Darley raised her finger in the air, 'rather than receiving the welcome Inanna had expected from Her sister, she was immediately struck to the ground, where Ereshkigal placed the Eye of Death upon Her.'

'Oh no,' I said, 'how awful.'

'It'll be OK,' Lucy whispered.

'Oh Lucy, don't spoil it,' said Rose.

'I'm not,' said Lucy, 'I just don't want her to be sad.'

'And for that I'm grateful,' I said smiling. 'So what happened next?'

'Well, under Erishkigal's instructions, Inanna's corpse was immediately hung upon a hook on the wall, where it stayed for three days and three nights. On the fourth day, being concerned that Inanna, had not returned to the Great Above, the faithful Ninshubur went as instructed to Inanna's father, Sin, the Moon God, to ask for help, but Sin refused.'

'Why did he say no?' I asked.

'Because it was never considered wise to mess with the decisions of the Underworld Gods,' said Mrs Darley.

'You'd have saved me though, wouldn't you Dad?' Lucy said turning to Bod.

'Of course I would.' Bod leaned over to tousle her hair.

'Well, Lucy, I'm afraid Inanna wasn't so lucky. Sin refused to help, so the faithful Ninshubur had to look elsewhere for assistance, and decided to go to wise Enki, God of the Deep Waters.'

'And did Enki help?' I asked, for now I was thoroughly swept up in this strange tale.

Mrs Darley nodded. 'He made two creatures from the dirt beneath his fingernails, whom he called 'The Galatur'.

'Yuk,' said Lucy, immediately inspecting her own fingernails for signs of the Galatur.

Mrs Darley continued her story. 'Now, to one Galatur, Enki gave the water of life, whilst to the other, he gave the food of life, and he instructed them to enter the Underworld unnoticed, like flies. He told them that once inside, they would find Ereshkigal, Queen of the Underworld about to give birth. Enki advised the Galatur to be sympathetic to her labour pains, for she would then offer them a gift of their choosing.'

'I can't imagine what sort of gift you would choose to take from the Queen of the Underworld,' I said shuddering.

'It's the body,' Lucy whispered.

'Lucy...' said Rose, looking at me apologetically.

'Lucy's quite right,' said Mrs Darley. 'Enki told the Galatur to only ask for the corpse that hung from the hook on the wall, and once it was in their possession, one of them was to sprinkle it with the food of life, whilst the other was to sprinkle it with the water of life, hence Inanna would miraculously return from the dead. And so...'

On cue, we all stood up, and with a slight alteration to the words, we chorused and mimed. 'From the Great Above, the Galatur opened their ears to the Great Below, and abandoned heaven and earth to descend into the Underworld.' I began to feel I was getting the hang of this.

'And so,' said Mrs Darley as we all sat down, 'everything happened exactly as the wise Enki had predicted, and having been sprinkled with both the water and food of life, Inanna once again returned to the Great Above, which provided the Sumerians with an explanation as to why the Moon disappeared from the sky for three nights each month and then returned again as a brand-new crescent.'

'Oh, I love that,' I said, 'and I can understand, Lucy, why this is your favourite story, especially with all the audience participation.'

'There's more to come, though isn't there?' Lucy turned to Mrs Darley.

'There is indeed,' she smiled, 'for no one can simply depart from the Underworld without leaving someone in his or her place, and therefore a suitable replacement was demanded by the Underworld Deities.'

'Oh no,' I said, 'not the poor Galatur? Not after they had been brave-enough to rescue her?'

Mrs Darley shook her head. 'No, the Galatur were safe. The Underworld deities initially suggested the faithful Ninshibur, she who had raised the alarm when Inanna failed to return to the Great Above, but Inanna refused. Then they asked for Inanna's sons, but again She refused.'

I was beginning to think we were running out of options as Mrs Darley continued. 'So, upon Her return from the

Great Below, Inanna went to visit Her lover, the shepherd Dumuzi whom She loved with all Her heart, to tell him She was still alive, and to ask for his advice as to who should be Her replacement in the underworld. But... when She finally caught up with Dumuzi out in the fields with his sheep, She saw that rather than being dressed in the dark colours of mourning, as She would have expected, he was wearing brightly coloured clothes, and was going about his business as usual.'

'Oh dear,' said Bod laughing, 'bad move.'

'Bad move indeed,' said Mrs Darley, joining in his laughter, 'for, out of anger, Inanna immediately suggested that the Underworld deities might like to take Dumuzi in Her place.'

Lucy smiled at me reassuringly. 'It's going to be okay though.'

'It is certainly going to be okay as Lucy put it,' said Mrs Darley, 'for Dumuzi's sister, Geshtinanna, begged the Underworld deities to let her share her beloved brother's time in the Underworld. And so, for six months of the year, Geshtinanna took Dumuzi's place, whilst he was released back to the world and returned to the arms of Inanna.'

'Ah, that's lovely,' I sighed.

'And of course,' said Mrs Darley, 'this part of the story provided the Sumerians with an explanation as to why the Earth lapsed into a quiet time of rest and retreat for one half of the year, before the new life returned once again.'

'What a wonderful story to explain both the seasons and the dark Moon as you called it,' I said. 'I will certainly take more notice of the Moon's phases in the future.'

'Well you can't really practice magick without being aware of them,' said Mrs Darley, rising from her chair and refilling our whiskey glasses.

'No, I'm sure you can't.' I said, feeling somewhat uneasy

at this sudden mention of magick yet again.

Moon Myth and Legend

The Moon is undoubtedly beautiful, and regardless of millennia of painstaking study by scientists, geologists and astronomers, She remains a beguiling enigma. Despite knowing that man has walked upon Her surface and brought back hard geological evidence that She is simply a rocky satellite that orbits our planet, does little to detract from Her numinous qualities.

When Neil Armstrong and Buzz Aldrin first walked on the surface of the Moon, they were almost lost for words as they attempted to comprehend not only the enormity of the task they had just accomplished, but also the stark beauty that surrounded them. Buzz Aldrin eventually described it as, 'magnificent desolation'.

The lives of the three astronauts who piloted Apollo 11 were understandably changed through their profound experience, and with less than twenty hours to go until splash down in the Pacific Ocean, Buzz Aldrin was quoted as saying:

'....as we've been discussing the events that have taken place in the past two or three days here on board our spacecraft, we've come to the conclusion that this has been far more than three men on a voyage to the Moon, more still than the efforts of a government and industry team – more, even, than the efforts of one nation. We feel that this stands as a symbol of the insatiable curiosity of all mankind to explore the unknown...'

For thousands of years before the race into space began however, the Moon had captured the imagination of mankind, inspiring works of art, poetry and prose. It therefore comes as little surprise that many Moon myths and legends have evolved with regards to its creation, behaviour, sexuality, residents and the deities who have become associated with it.

Sumerian Moon Myths

Around 5,000 years ago, the Sumerians, who occupied the area of the world we now know as Iraq and Kuwait, formed one of the first urban city-states known as Ur.

The citizens of Ur held the Moon in great esteem. Every month at the sighting of the new Moon, they held a feast in their Great Temple, the *Ziggurat of Nanna*, to honour their Moon God, who, despite being recognised as a masculine force, also took on a triple aspect.

At the first sighting of the crescent Moon, they worshipped Him as Suen or Sin. When the Moon became full, they worshipped Him as Nanna, one of the oldest deities in the Mesopotamian pantheon, and at the dark Moon phase, they honoured Him as Asimbabbar. Over time, these three aspects merged, and Sin became the triumphant Sumerian Moon God, to whom a feast was dedicated each month upon the sighting of the new crescent.

Sin was often depicted as an old man riding a bull, with a beard of lapis lazuli and a headdress of four horns surmounted by the crescent Moon. In addition to being revered as the Moon God, He was also worshipped as the deity of the cattle herds of the lower Euphrates River, and as such, a popular cult soon developed. Within the cult, Sin was depicted as a bull at the full Moon with an orb upon His forehead, and as a calf at the new Moon with a crescent Moon upon His head.

Sin had a holy mountain dedicated to Him called Mount Sinai, or Moon Mountain, and according to legend, it was upon this mountain that Divine Law was received and given to the people of Sumeria. This story will be undoubtedly familiar, for in the Biblical Old Testament, we are told that Mount Sinai is the mountain upon which Moses received the Ten Commandments from Yahweh. These commandments outlined the moral laws by which the people of Israel should live, and also provided guidelines on how to worship their new God.

The third of these commandments stated: *'Thou shalt not make unto thee any graven image'*, but whilst Moses was on Mount Sinai, receiving the commandments from his new God, his people, who were gathered in the valley below, became tired of waiting, and reverted to their old practices of worship.

Upon descending from Mount Sinai, Moses was horrified to discover that with the approval of his brother, Aaron, the people had melted down their gold jewellery to create an image of Sin in his new Moon aspect as a calf. The Bible tells us in Exodus 32:19-21:

'When Moses approached the camp and saw the calf and the dancing, his anger burned and he threw the tablets out of his hands, breaking them to pieces at the foot of the mountain. And he took the calf they had made and burned it in the fire; then he ground it to powder, scattered it on the water and made the Israelites drink it.

He said to Aaron, "What did these people do to you, that you led them into such great sin?"'

Today, the word 'sin' has a firm place in the English language, and is described in the Concise Oxford Dictionary as:

'The breaking of a divine, or moral law, especially by a conscious act'.

Interestingly, the word 'sin', still remains the Syrian and Kurdish name for the Moon.

Sumerian legends tell of the Moon God, Sin, being born from the rape of His mother, Ninlil, Goddess of the Grain, by the Air God, Enlil. As a punishment, Enlil was banished to the Underworld, but Ninlil decided to follow him and allow him to witness the birth of his child.

When a child is born in the Underworld however, he or she cannot leave, and automatically comes under the guardianship of the Underworld deities. Enlil, desperate for his first born to be returned to the upper world, made a bargain with the Underworld deities saying that he would willingly give up his next three children, on condition that his first born, Sin, could go free and light the night skies.

The Underworld deities agreed to Enlil's request, providing the Sumerians with an explanation of why the Moon came to illuminate the night sky. When a lunar eclipse occurred however, and the face of the Moon darkened to blood red, the Sumerians believed that their Moon God, Sin, was being attacked by the Underworld deities, and in order to restore the Moon to His former brilliance, the Sumerian kings would ritually wash themselves. They believed this would appease the dark gods and purify the Moon, enabling Him to shine brightly once more in the night sky.

Moon Time

The Moon was once the sole time piece of ancient man, and the first measure of Moon time was probably taken as the new crescent rose between natural markers set within the landscape, such as hills or trees.

As man evolved, stone temples were built to capture the movement of the Moon, as can be evidenced from many ancient monuments all over the world. The standing stone circle of Stenness in the Orkney Isles, is still referred to as 'The Temple of the Moon'.

In 1974, the archaeologist Alexander Thom, put forward the theory that Stonehenge was built in three phases over a period of 2,000 years, beginning in 3,100BCE, and was originally an observatory for studying the movements of the Moon.

The original Roman month was also governed by the Moon, and like their Greek counterparts, the Romans employed a 'Moon Watcher' to sit on a hill and blow a trumpet at the first sight of the new crescent, allowing the following month's festivals to then be arranged. This first day of the month was known as the *Kalendae*, and is the root of our word, calendar.

There is therefore, evidence for the Moon being used as a time piece up to 5,000 years ago, but archaeological explorations that began in 1879 and continued up until the 1940's, were to shed new light on just how ancient a time piece the Moon actually was.

During this period, many caves were discovered in Northern Europe, including the famous caves of Lascaux in the Dordogne in France. These caves not only contained beautiful cave paintings, but also figures, tools and pieces of bone with a bewildering array of markings carved upon them, dating back some 30,000 years to the Palaeolithic period.

These objects were removed and taken to museums across Europe where they lay, almost forgotten, in glass cases, until 1965, when a man called Alexander Marshack began re-examining the finds, and asked the question, 'Could the marks upon some of these ancient objects actually mean something?'

After taking one piece of bone in particular, which had been discovered in the Abri Blanchard in the Dordogne, and comparing it to other similar pieces, Marshack finally concluded that the carvings represented a primitive representation of two months of the Moon's cycle.

Subsequent findings from Africa, Russia and Czechoslovakia, confirmed Marshack's initial theories, and he went on to suggest that these markings could mark the beginning of man's cognitive thought process. This early understanding of the relationship between the Moon and the measurement of time, could have paved the way for the subsequent development of writing, mathematics, astronomy, agriculture, and chronology itself.

Due to the importance given to the Moon over thousands of years, in both the marking of time and the celebration of certain religious festivals, She has understandably made Her way into many sacred texts:

'God created the Moon and appointed its 'houses' in order that men might know the number of years and the measure of time.'
(The Koran Sura x 5)

'He made the Moon also to serve in her season for a declaration of times, and a sign of the world. From the Moon is the sign of feasts, a light that decreaseth in her perfection. The month is called after her name increasing wonderfully in her changing.'
(Ecclesiasticus 43: 6-8)

'The Moon marks off the seasons and the sun knows when to go down.'
(Psalms 104: 19)

In later times, the Moon continued to exercise Her magick over many great writers, including Shakespeare, as illustrated in the following extract from Romeo and Juliet (Act 2, Scene ii):

Romeo: *Lady, by yonder blessed moon I swear,*
              That tips with silver all these fruit-tree tops.

Juliet: *Oh swear not by the moon, the inconsistent moon,*
              That monthly changes in her circled orb,
              Lest that thy love prove likewise variable.

In early times, the lunar month was simply divided into two parts, and known by several names. The people of Africa referred to them as the 'light and dark' halves, the Hindus referred to them as 'waxing and waning', whilst the Peruvians preferred 'waking and sleeping', The Celts meanwhile divided these waxing and waning phases into two, two-week periods, or 'fourteen nights of the Moon', which eventually gave us the word 'fortnight'.

Gradually a third phase, that of the full Moon was added and eventually a fourth phase was introduced, that of the dark or new Moon, thus dividing the month into four distinct periods, albeit not exactly even.

In Babylonia, the day of the full Moon was once taken as a day of rest, but as time passed, these rest days gradually increased to one day in every seven, where they were known as 'Evil Days' or 'Moon Days', with the latter providing the origin of our word, 'Monday'. Hence the twenty-eight-day Moon cycle, or month, was divided into four smaller periods of seven days, or a week, with the word 'week' deriving from the Old English, *wice,* meaning turning, change, or succession.

Early man learned therefore to mark out the seasons by the Moon, so that he might know when to hunt, gather, retreat and rest, and as such, he gave each Moon a name which was in keeping with what was happening in nature. Many cultures followed a similar pattern, resulting in a myriad of names depending on their place in the world.

Initially, this system worked well, but the lunar year was always going to be eleven days short of the solar year, and as time passed, these twelve named Moons began to fall out of sync with what was happening in the natural world. For example, the Sap or Seed Moon, which originally referred to the early spring Moon, may have appeared in late winter when snow was on the ground. Therefore, in an attempt to bring the Moons and the seasons back into harmony, an extra Moon was added thus making a year of thirteen Moons (364 days).

The table below lists just a few of the many names given to the thirteen new Moons of the year, dependent on location and culture, and begins with the first Moon following the 'Dark Time' (Winter Solstice). The dates given are simply a guide to help the reader equate them with our modern calendar.

Dates between which the New Moon falls	Old Medieval English and Celtic Moon Names	Native American Moon Names From various tribes	Wiccan or Neo-Pagan Moon Names
21 December 18 January	Old Quiet Wolf	Cold Cooking Winter Wolf	Ice Wolf
19 January 15 February	Ice Snow Storm	Bony Hunger Little Famine Snow Trapper's	Chaste Hunger Snow Storm

16 February 15 March	Chaste Lenten Lengthening Plough Wind	Big Famine Chaste Fish Wind Worm	Death Sap
16 March 12 April	Budding Egg Growing New Shoot Seed	Awakening Flower Pink Planter's Wildcat	Awakening Seed
13 April 10 May	Bright Hare Milk	Flower Milk Panther	Grass Hare
11 May 7 June	Dyan Flower Horse	Green Corn Rose Strawberry	Dyad Planting
8 June 5 July	Calm Hay Mead	Buck Crane Ripe Corn Summer	Blessing Honey Mead Rose
6 July 3 August	Corn Dispute	Dog Days Sturgeon Women's	Lightening Wyrt (Wort)
4 August 31 August	Grain Lynx	Barley Fruit	Harvest
1 September 28 September	Barley Fruit Singing Wine	Harvest Mulberry Nut Singing	Barley Wine

29 September 26 October	Blood Harvest	Blackberry Harvest Hunter's	Blood
27 October 23 November	Dark Hunter's	Beaver Sassafras Traveller's	Birch Tree
24 November 21 December	Cold Oak	Cold Peach Snow	Long Night Oak

This rough method of arranging time continued to be a problem, and it was clear that a more precise solution needed to be found that would synchronise solar and lunar time. It would however, be many centuries before the problem was finally resolved.

Even the Egyptians were having trouble with their calendar. They decided to have a thirty-day month and a twelve-month year, but this only added up to 360 days, which left them five days short. Hence the following story of Thoth, the Egyptian Moon God, was told to explain the anomaly.

Thoth challenged the Moon to a game of draughts and upon being successful, the Moon gave Thoth five extra days. These days became 'sacred days', or 'days out of time', which basically did not count and were celebrated as holy days, marking the birth of notable Egyptian gods and goddesses, namely: Isis, Osiris, Seth, Nephthys and Aruelis.

In ancient Greece, they simply added a month every two years, whilst in Rome, the first *fasti*, literally meaning a 'register of days', or calendar, was published in 304BCE. This calendar showed that the Roman year began in March, so any days that needed to be added were slotted in at the end of their year in February. During the Republic however, the authorities sometimes could not be bothered to add the required number of days, and as a result, the calendar sank deeper and deeper into chaos, until in 45BCE, Julius Caesar decided to address the problem.

During that year, Caesar brought in a man called Sosigenes, an Alexandrian astronomer, to adapt the old Egyptian system which was based on the solar year. Using his best calculations, Sosigenes suggested that a year should be 365.25 days long, and that with effect from 44BCE, each year should be extended to 365 days, with an extra day to be added every fourth year. In order to begin afresh however, he had to extend 43BCE to 445 days.

Interestingly, the mystical phrase often used in fairy tales to describe a passing period of time is 'a year and a day', and probably derives from these slight adjustments to the calendar in ancient times.

The final alterations to our modern-day calendar were made in 1582, when Pope Gregory XIII oversaw changes to the Julian calendar, due to each year being eleven minutes too long. The revised 'Gregorian Calendar' therefore abolished eleven days, revised the leap years, and changed the beginning of the year from 1st March to the 1st January.

This new calendar however, was not introduced everywhere at the same time, and was not adopted in England until 1752. This was down to public resistance, brought about by the fact that it had been designed by a Catholic Pope. The implementation of the new calendar was certainly not a popular decision, especially with the citizens of Bristol, who rioted in the streets saying that not only had they been done out of eleven days of wages, but also eleven days of life.

It may have seemed that solar time had finally superceded lunar time, but deep within the English countryside, where despite Christianity being the religion of the land, the old ways still held sway, and the lunar year of thirteen Moons was still used to celebrate many festivals. This is evidenced in the fourteenth century folk rhyme, '*The Ballard* (sic) *of Robin Hood and the Curtal Friar*', mentioned in Robert Graves book, '*The White Goddess.*'

> *'But how many merry months be in the yeare?*
> *There are thirteen, I say;*
> *The mid-summer moon is the merryest of all,*
> *Next to the merry month of May.'*

Sadly however, just as lunar time was pushed out by solar time, this rhyme too was rewritten to 'fit in' with the modern world. Thus it became:

> *'There are twelve months in all the year*
> *As I hear many men say.*
> *But the merriest month in all the year*
> *Is the merry month of May.'*

For secular purposes, the modern world calendar is organised by solar time, but as far as the sacred calendar is concerned, many parts of the world still adhere to the lunar year, including the Jewish and Muslim traditions.

The Hebrew calendar (based on the earlier Babylonian one), has twelve or thirteen months, each beginning with the new Moon. The resulting discrepancy of eleven days between lunar and solar time is resolved by slipping in a leap year that contains an extra month, seven times in every nineteen years. This ensures that the Feast of the Passover always falls at the full Moon in the spring.

Prayers are always recited at each new Moon, and during the celebration, everyone is informed of the exact moment of the new Moon. If it can be seen in the night sky three days following its birth, then a ceremony of 'sanctification' is carried out outdoors, called *Kiddush Levanah,* where each person greets the other with the words, *'shalom aleikhem',* meaning 'Peace be upon you'.

In 634CE, Muhammad declared that the Islamic year should consist of twelve lunar months, simply counted from one new Moon to the next. The Islamic year therefore begins eleven days earlier each year, resulting in ninety-seven Islamic years roughly equating to a hundred solar years. This means that the Islamic festivals move around the seasonal year, and come back into line once in every thirty-three years. The crescent Moon can be seen on top of each mosque minaret, and for the past 200 years has also been depicted on the Islamic flag.

Even when a culture or religion adheres strictly to solar time, certain festivals are still calculated by the phase of the Moon, including most of the Buddhist festivals, which are held either at the full or new Moon. These Moons are regarded as times of strength and spiritual power, and also acknowledge the fact that Buddha achieved enlightenment at the time of the full Moon.

The Christian religion also calculates the date of its most important festival, Easter, by the Moon. Although Easter is usually celebrated on the Sunday after the full Moon, following the Spring Equinox, rather than on the day of the full Moon itself, a formula that was agreed upon at the Council of Nicaea in 325CE.

Occasionally however, this formula is known to vary due to the fact that the church always calculates the date of the Spring Equinox as being 21st March, rather than acknowledging its true date, which can fall any time between the 19th and 23rd March, according to the exact moment that the plane of Earth's equator passes through the centre of the

Sun's disk.

Interestingly, the Saxon Goddess, Eostre or Ostara, after whom (we are told by the Venerable Bede), Easter takes its name, was honoured on the actual day of the full Moon following the Spring Equinox.

It was not only the ancients however, who measured time, celebrated their festivals, and stood in wonder beneath our evocative nightly visitor, for in many ways we too, still yield to Her call. I learned from Mrs Darley that each Moon offers us not only the opportunity to align ourselves with what is happening in nature, but also helps us to connect with the ancestors and avail of their lunar wisdom.

Mrs Darley Tale: The Wine Moon

It was one of those rare times I treasured, when there was just me and Mrs Darley, sitting around the fireside in her cottage. A vase of fragrant herbs stood on the hearth, against which was propped the face of a green man moulded from clay, and beside it, an elegant statue of a Maiden Goddess, all reminiscent of the beautiful season of Beltane which had just passed.

Without a word, Mrs Darley suddenly stood up and opened the cupboard in the fireside alcove beside her chair - the 'secret cupboard' as I liked to call it. On special occasions, this was the place from which the Irish Poteen seemed to materialise. I fervently hoped however, that for this evening at least, the Poteen would stay well-hidden, for I had an early appointment the following morning.

I need not have worried, for Mrs Darley simply produced a beautifully rounded blue glass bottle and placed it on the table between us, along with two glasses.

She then disappeared briefly into the kitchen, before returning with two dishes containing a generous slice of cherry pie, accompanied by a large bowl of Cornish clotted cream. As she set the dishes down, she turned her attention to the blue bottle and began to pour the most beautiful rich, purple liquid into our glasses. I was fascinated by it. Indeed I was not entirely sure I had ever drunk anything that colour before.

Taking her seat once more, she leaned forward and held up her glass. 'To our time together my dear, on the night of the full Dyad Moon.'

Not being quite sure what we were toasting, I nevertheless echoed Mrs Darley's words and took a sip of the purple liquid. It was the most heavenly thing I had ever tasted.

'Mmm,' I sighed. 'That is pure nectar.'

She smiled. 'I'm glad you like it. It's homemade damson wine from last year. I always make some sort of alcoholic beverage during the Wine Moon in September. This year's will be plum wine, as Phyllis assures me her trees will be laden with fruit.'

'Well, I'll certainly look forward to trying it, especially if it's as delicious as this.'

'And I will look forward to sharing it with you,' said Mrs Darley.

As our conversation regarding Mrs Darley's homemade wines and the specific Moon under which it was made came to a close, I thought I would take advantage of the moment and question her further on what to me was a fascinating subject.

'I remember you telling me a few months ago, that each of the Moons once had a name, but what did you say this month's Moon was called again?'

'The late May Moon is called the Dyad Moon.'

'What does that mean?'

'Well, the word Dyad, means a pair, or two, and refers to the fact that at this time of year, the constellation of Gemini, the twins, is present in the night sky, which comprises of the twin stars of Castor and Pollux.'

'Ah, that makes sense,' I said, 'so presumably the Wine Moon is so-called because the ancients made some sort of drink at that time?'

'Well in actual fact, the Celts probably made their wine beneath the Wort Moon in July, when the warm weather would aid fermentation. For them, the Wine Moon actually represented a time of divination, and was believed to be the Moon most favoured and blessed by their gods. But in order to avail themselves of the gift of divine prophecy, the Celts often consumed mind altering substances – wine amongst them - through which they were able to access other realms, and tonight that's exactly what we will do.'

She must have noticed the look of concern on my face. 'Oh, not the drink dear, just the prophecy.' She scooped a generous serving of clotted cream onto her pie. 'Tell me, what do you understand by the term divination?'

I wasn't quite sure what to say and was a little wary of making a fool of myself. 'Foretelling the future in some way?' I offered hesitantly.

'Well that is certainly a common belief. However, I like to look upon it a little differently. You see, whether we realise it or not, deep within each one of us, lie all the answers we need to overcome life's challenges.'

I laughed. 'I'm not so sure of that.'

'Oh but they do. It's just that most of us have forgotten how to retrieve the information. For me, *that* is what divination is really all about and regardless of its form, it simply acts as a signpost that points us to the answers we seek. The route we ultimately choose however, always remains our decision.'

'So nothing is set in stone?' I asked.

Mrs Darley shook her head. 'No. Divination, my dear, is

merely a tool that allows us to turn our attention inward, so that we might make contact with that part of ourselves we know is there, yet seldom connect with. I suppose you could call it, 'contacting the soul'. Does that make sense?'

I nodded, feeling more at ease now and eagerly awaiting whatever this evening would bring, rather than being my usual apprehensive self.

'We will use the Runes,' she said, putting down her now empty dish and standing up to reach for a black velvet bag that hung on a hook beside the granite pillar of the fireplace.

'The Runes?'

'Yes.' She tipped a few of the bag's contents out on the little coffee table. 'The Runes were the written alphabet of the Norse and other Germanic peoples before the adoption of the Latin alphabet in the late Middle Ages.'

I looked at the strange symbols which were inscribed on what looked like small clay tablets. 'But how can an alphabet become a method of divination?' I asked.

'Because each symbol or letter possesses a meaning far beyond its face value,' Mrs Darley replied. 'In fact, the word 'Rune' actually means both letter and secret or mystery, which is why Odin, the Norse god, coveted them so much.'

'I've heard of Odin,' I said, 'but I don't really know too much about him.'

'According to the *Hávamál,* a Norse poem that forms part of the *Poetic Edda,* Odin was the chief deity of the Nordic gods.'

'Like Zeus was to the Greeks?'

'Yes,' said Mrs Darley, 'and being the chief deity, you may think that Odin would have everything he could wish for.'

'And he didn't?'

She shook her head. 'There was one thing Odin did not have and which he coveted above all else - knowledge of the Runes. For Odin was a relentless seeker of both wisdom and the mysteries of life, and was willing to sacrifice anything in order to obtain such a gift.'

'But why couldn't he just have taken them if he was the chief deity?' I asked.

'Well Odin may have been the chief deity, but that didn't mean that there weren't more powerful entities at work.'

'But I thought the gods were all powerful.'

'Yes, to an extent they were, but in many cultures, the Norse included, people also believed in other beings that were both revered and feared, even by the gods.'

'Oh, I didn't know that.'

'At the centre of the Norse cosmos,' Mrs Darley continued, 'stood the tree of knowledge called Yggdrasil, which housed the nine Nordic worlds. Its upper branches supported Asgard, the home of Odin and the Aesir deities, whilst in its roots lay buried in the Well of Urd, a pool that was believed to be the home of the most powerful forces, amongst which dwelt the Norns.'

'I've definitely never heard of them.'

'You remember you mentioned the Greek God Zeus being the equivalent of the Norse God Odin earlier? Well, by the same token, the Norns are the Norse equivalent of the three Fates in Greek mythology, or Shakespeare's Wyrd Sisters. They are the ones who spin, weave, and ultimately cut the thread of life of all beings.'

'Ah yes,' I said, feeling I had suddenly reached more familiar ground, 'now the Wyrd Sisters, I *have* heard of.'

'Well, in order to shape the fate or destiny of any being residing in the nine worlds, the Norns would carve, with magickal intent, runic symbols into the trunk of the Yggdrasil tree, watched by Odin, who wished more than anything else to possess their power and wisdom.'

'Can't blame him for that.'

'Ah, being privy to such gifts isn't always a positive thing my dear, for with insight comes fearful images and great responsibility, and so you can appreciate that the Runes were not easily won.'

'So how did Odin actually manage to get the Runes?' I asked.

'Well, the *Hávamál* tells of Odin hanging on a windy tree, without food or drink for nine long nights, whilst also bearing a wound made by his own spear. Finally, and no doubt in a mind altered state, he not only spied and seized the Runes, but also began to have an innate understanding of their secrets and wisdom.'

'So, through this self-imposed trial, he did actually manage to gain the insight he so wanted?'

Mrs Darley nodded. 'Thankfully he did, which means that we too can now benefit from Odin's hard-won wisdom through the reading of the Runes. You see sometimes my dear, in order to progress spiritually, we are asked to face certain challenges.'

I nodded. 'That makes sense'.

'Of course,' continued Mrs Darley, 'when we are actually faced with these challenges our initial reaction is often resistance, especially if we know our life will be harder because of it. Sacred law however, works in mysterious ways, and we should remember that the trial we are asked to undertake is often nothing compared to that which is gained.'

I didn't know what to say to that. It was something I had never really contemplated before.

'Come my dear,' said Mrs Darley, offering me the black velvet bag. 'Put your hand in here and take a moment to focus upon a particular issue in your life which either troubles you, or to which you would like an answer. Then, when you are ready, draw out a Rune and place it on the table. You will find that the right stone will somehow find its way into your hands.'

I did not have to think too hard about an issue I needed guidance with. Earlier that day at work, I had been given the opportunity to apply for a promotion, an easy enough decision to make on the surface, but the new job meant going through a tough selection process. If successful, I would then need to attend a six-week training course away from home, followed by exams, and only if I passed these, would I be able to start my new job.

The real problem was that if I failed at any stage, my current job (which I thoroughly enjoyed), would not be held open, and I would have to take whatever was offered, possibly at a lower grade.

The benefits of course, came by way of company car, a managerial position, and a much healthier salary, but was it worth the risk, the worry, and more to the point, would I be able to meet the tough targets that went with the job?

Conveying all these thoughts into the little velvet bag, I finally pulled out a Rune stone which, as Mrs Darley predicted, did indeed find its way easily into my hand. I placed it carefully on the table as Mrs Darley cleared away our empty dishes and replenished our glasses with the damson wine.

She then returned to her seat, and with her spectacles balanced rather precariously on the end of her nose, announced 'Ah, Thurisaz - the gateway.'

The Rune - Thurisaz

She paused for a moment as though carefully choosing her words. 'I see you standing on the threshold of a new life, and at this moment, you are unsure whether to take that step. You have confidence issues, you doubt your ability, you're probably thinking, "Better the devil you know," but remember my dear, nothing is accomplished in this life by playing it safe. Too many lives on this Earth have ended with thoughts of, "What if?" The decision however, is ultimately yours.'

I nodded. The accuracy of her words left me reeling.

'I feel that perhaps the Runes have opened up your mind to new possibilities?' Mrs Darley asked gently as she replaced the stone in the velvet bag.

'What you just told me… it's just so appropriate…'
She leaned forward and patted my hand. 'Well, my dear, the Runes have spoken, the gateway lies open and the Dyad Moon lights your path, all you have to do is have the courage to step through.'

The following poem, 'She, was inspired through contemplating the fact that both a beautiful lover, and a beautiful Moon, have the power to seduce...

She

I am the seductress,
The temptress,
The enchantress.

The sight of my face
Promises promiscuous pleasures,
For I am the jewel of the heavens
Against which all else pales.

I am the mistress of the night.

Chapter Three

Moon Phases

Mrs Darley Tale: The Moonstone

Picking up the post from the floor of the porch on my return from work one June evening, I was surprised to see a note in Mrs Darley's elegant handwriting, and wondered why she had chosen to write to me.

Hello dear,
Just to let you know that Phyllis has sprained her wrist, so I'm spending a couple of days with her, to make sure she's OK.
Hope you're free on Thursday, as we're all gathering to watch the lunar eclipse in the garden. It's not due until around 1am though, so for those who don't have the stamina, or desire to stay up, we're holding a small ritual a little earlier.
Would you like to come around about 10pm? Wrap up warm if it's a chilly night and bring a torch and a small, clean, empty bottle.
Mrs D

I had never seen a lunar eclipse, and knew little about them, so I was very much looking forward to it. I smiled to myself as I placed the note on the table, for I loved these invitations into Mrs Darley's magical world, and although I couldn't imagine the reason for taking a small clean bottle, I knew that my Thursday night out with a few people from work, would now take second place to this irresistible alternative.

***

As Thursday evening closed in, and the Sun disappeared behind Sharp Tor, the sky remained beautifully clear, providing a wonderful backdrop for the majestic skyline of Dartmoor. As always however, a coolness descended on the high moor, and taking Mrs Darley's advice, I had changed my tee shirt and cotton trousers for a jumper and jeans.

At ten o clock, just as night was beginning to swallow the day, I collected a torch, picked up my bottle and made my way round to Mrs Darley's cottage. Here, I found a group of familiar faces, who were fast becoming my favourite people, waiting on the small patch of grass outside the front door.

Bod, Rose, and Phyllis were accompanied by Don (whom I fondly referred to as my hippie next door neighbour), Eddie, the kind and literal 'poacher turned game keeper', who had come to my rescue with a van on the day I moved into my little cottage, and Peter, whose relationship with Mrs Darley I suspected (although I had no evidence), was a little more than platonic.

'Hello, dear.' Mrs Darley greeted me warmly. 'I think we're all here now, so come on everyone, off we go.'

Feeling somewhat surprised that we were leaving the confines of the cottages, I found myself walking along with Phyllis.

'How's your wrist now?' I asked.

'Oh, still a little painful, but so much better than it was – at least I have some use back, and can manage to get dressed and boil a kettle.'

'That's good to hear,' I said. 'So tell me Phyllis, where are we going tonight exactly?'

'To the Moon Stone.'

The Moon Stone meant nothing to me, but before I had chance to ask her for an explanation, we turned off the lane and onto the little path which led down into the wooded copse adjacent to the cottages. Here Eddie helped Phyllis to cross what was, in the rapidly growing darkness, very uneven ground.

Suddenly, we all came to a halt beside an enormous granite boulder, unusually rounded in shape, which I had seen many times on my walks through the copse.

Mrs Darley nimbly climbed up onto the boulder to address us. 'Gather round everyone, and switch off your torches, for the moonlight will be sufficient for now.'

I noticed that to one side of her stood two pillar candles, one of silver and the other red, contained within large glass jars, whilst in front of them was a beautiful pewter chalice, and beside it, a heavy pewter dish.

'Here we are once more at the Moon Stone, to acknowledge the night of the lunar eclipse, under this, the full Blessing Moon.

'I know that for many of you this is a familiar occasion, although sometimes we are not so fortunate as to be able to see the eclipse, due to the fact that they often occur during daylight or other inconvenient times.'

'Not tonight though, eh, Mrs D?' Said Bod.

'No Bod, not tonight. Tonight we are indeed blessed, and following our ceremony, we will return to the garden to watch this spectacle together. Meanwhile, for those of you who have not experienced such an event before, I hope our little ritual brings you many blessings.'

At this point, Mrs Darley bent down to light the candles and then, jumping lightly down from the Moon Stone, took the chalice in her left hand.

On cue, Eddie lifted down the heavy pewter dish and began to fill the chalice with what looked like liquid gold in the light of the Moon.

When the chalice was full, Mrs Darley turned to each of us in turn, bidding us take a drink as she moved around the circle speaking the words:

> *'Sacred Lady, bless our mead,*
> *Sacred mead, bless our lips,*
> *Sacred lips bless our Lady.'*

When we had all partaken of what I can only describe as a drink fit for the gods, she replaced the chalice on the boulder and stepped back up onto the Moon Stone. Raising her arms to the sky, she turned her face to the Moon.

'As the Blessing Moon shines in our skies,' she said, 'so may She also shine in our lives. And when Her silver orb becomes bloodied in the shadow of the Earth, so we will journey with Her through the darkness, before finally bathing together once again in Her light. Blessed be our Lady Moon.'

'Blessed be our Lady Moon,' we repeated in unison.

Everyone stood in silence, lost in the beauty of the moment, until Mrs Darley finally stepped down from the Moon Stone, and taking the goblet once more from its resting place, she carefully began to fill the little bottles we had brought with us.

Taking my bottle, she curled her hand around mine. 'This, my dear, is honeyed mead, which has been blessed beneath our Honeyed Moon. Use it wisely and it will bring you many riches. Drink of it when you have need of courage, of comfort and of guidance, especially in the aftermath of a lunar eclipse, when periods of transformation and movement are often experienced.'

She must have noticed my rather worried expression. 'Forward movement is good. It is the only way, and is the one constant in our uncertain world. So my dear, tonight, when the bloodied Moon visits our skies, and the winds of change rustle the leaves on the trees, drink in the blessings of this Honeyed Moon to fortify your soul and strengthen your spirit.'

Moon Phases

The majority of us have, at some point in our lives, been bewitched by the moonlight, despite the fact that the Moon does not actually radiate its own light, but borrows it from the Sun, just as the Earth does. This is made possible by the fact that as the Earth moves around the Sun and the Moon moves around the Earth, the light of the Sun falls at increasing and decreasing angles upon the face of the Moon, resulting in what we term 'phases'.

We have seen that the ancients measured time by roughly dividing these phases into four, each lasting on average seven days. Namely:

- New to first quarter
- First quarter to full
- Full to second quarter
- Second quarter to new.

Today these phases have been broken down further, albeit they can vary according to differing points of view, but in the main include:

- New Moon
- Waxing Crescent
- First Quarter
- Waxing Gibbous

- Full Moon
- Waning Gibbous
- Second Quarter
- Waning Crescent
- Dark Moon

Please note: Some will see dark Moon and new Moon as one and the same phase.

Moon Phase	Visible Features of the Moon
New Moon	This is a 'Day Moon', as it rises around dawn and sets just after sunset. It is notoriously difficult to see, especially during the first 24-48 hours, due to the powerful light from the Sun. The record for someone spotting the new Moon was set in 1916, and was just 14.5 hours after its 'birth'. When it becomes visible, it is a slender crescent shaped like a backwards 'C' (this is reversed in the Southern Hemisphere.) This is the only phase of the Moon during which a solar eclipse occurs. See image No.1
Waxing Crescent	This is when we begin to notice the beautiful crescent as it rises approximately fifty minutes later each day and lingers in the night sky that little longer, growing and gaining in size and light as it does so. As we look at the waxing Moon, we can see a distinct dark circle about a third of the way down close to the outer edge, known as the Sea of Crises (Mare Crisium), whilst beneath this a larger dark shape becomes noticeable known as the Sea of Fertility (Mare Fecunditatis). See image No. 2

First Quarter	At the first quarter, the Moon rises around midday and sets around midnight. Interestingly however, for one day around the time of the first quarter, the Moon does not actually rise and set on the same day, due to its setting time being after midnight. The Moon is now shaped like a 'D' and further 'seas' are revealed closer to the straight line of the 'D'. These include the Sea of Serenity (Mare Serenitatis), closest to the top of the Moon as we look at it, adjoining it below, is the Sea of Tranquillity (Mare Tranquillitatis), and beneath this lies the Sea of Nectar (Mare Nectaris). See image No. 3
Waxing Gibbous	The term 'gibbous' derives from the Latin word gibbosus meaning 'humpbacked' and refers to its rather odd shape between the quarter and full Moon, where the Moon is neither 'D' shaped nor round. The waxing gibbous Moon appears in our skies during the afternoon, and sets in the early hours of the morning. During this phase, the second half of the Moon comes into view and we can see towards the top of the Moon, part of the large Sea of Rains (Mare Imbrium), below which is the Seething Bay (Sinus Aestuum). Alongside this and a little towards the centre is the Sea of Vapours (Mare Vaporum), whilst below all of these, sits the Sea of Clouds (Mare Nubicum). See image No 4.
Full Moon	This is the Moon's most awaited phase, where the sky is flooded with a ghostly luminescence and She is revealed in all Her glory. Rising as the Sun sets, the full Moon is with us throughout the night, setting around Sun rise at dawn.

	Although we are now able to see the full face of the Moon, the light detracts from the clarity of her features. Nevertheless, the western side of the Moon now shows us the Ocean of Storms (Oceanus Procellarum) and the Sea of Moisture (Mare Humorum). Visible at the northern tip of the Moon is a long slender strip known as the Sea of Cold (Mare Frigoris) and to the west of this the Bay of Dew (Sinus Roris). The Sea of Rains now extends into the decidedly smaller Bay of Rainbows (Sinus Iridium) and a dark spot on its northern edge is also visible, this being a crater of some considerable depth named after Plato. This is the only Moon phase during which a full lunar eclipse can occur. See image No 5
Waning Gibbous	The Moon now begins her descent into the darkness and the waning gibbous Moon slips into the shadows on the eastern side, this being opposite to its earlier waxing phase. The Sea of Crises (Mare Crisium) now disappears from view. See image No 6
Second Quarter	The second quarter Moon is shaped like a backwards 'D', being a mirror image of the first quarter. The Seas of Serenity, Tranquillity and Nectar now fall into darkness and are no longer visible. There is a day around this phase that the Moon fails to rise, due to it rising just after midnight, although generally the last quarter Moon rises before midnight and sets around midday. See image No 7.

Waning Crescent	The waning crescent is a mirror image of the waxing crescent as the Moon now appears as a perfect 'C'. The only sea that remains visible is that of the Ocean of Storms (Oceanus Procellarum). This Moon is only visible in the east just before sunrise, as the bright sunlight soon makes it fade into obscurity, although in reality the Moon stays in the sky until late afternoon. See image No 8.
Dark Moon	To some, this phase is a misnomer and the waning crescent simply becomes the waxing crescent once again. To the naked eye however, the Moon is rendered invisible for two to three days, due to the waning and waxing crescents being so slender that the Sun's light completely obscures them from view, hence the term, 'Dark Moon'. See image No 1.

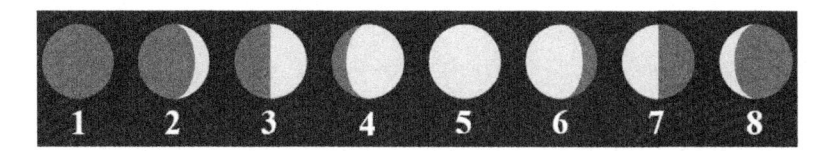

Images 1-8 By Pamplelune - Own work, CC BY-SA 3.0, https://commons.wikimedia.org/w/index.php?curid=4314744

Rare Lunar events

The Moon is a strange creature which has, over the centuries, been likened to a woman, both with regards to Her cyclic nature, and Her unpredictability. She constantly reminds us that just when we think we have all Her anomalies worked out, She is still the Queen of mystery and intrigue.

Lunar Eclipse:

For the ancients, a lunar eclipse must have instilled feelings of terror and fear, bestowing upon us a legacy of folklore and superstition. Today of course, we have a scientific explanation as to why and how an eclipse occurs, but nevertheless it remains an event which still has the power to make us stop and ponder upon its meaning.

A lunar eclipse occurs when the Sun, Moon and Earth lie in a straight line. If the Earth did not sit at a five-degree tilt in relation to the Moon's orbit, then a lunar eclipse would occur every month at the full Moon (likewise, there would also be an eclipse of the Sun at every new Moon). The tilt causes the Moon to pass either a fraction above or below the shadow of the Earth, thereby avoiding an eclipse.

Approximately twice a year however, the Sun, the Earth, and the Moon, find themselves in perfect alignment, resulting in the Moon passing through the Earth's shadow and bringing about the fascinating phenomenon of a lunar eclipse.

Little by little, the bright face of the Moon drains away and becomes veiled by a blood red orb. To the ancients, this terrifying event violated the natural order of things, and was therefore regarded as an omen of doom and despair. For them, the waning Moon was an accepted occurrence that formed part and parcel of nature's pattern, but an eclipse was something unnatural and outside the normal course of events.

The word 'eclipse', derives from the Greek ekleipsis meaning 'abandonment', which suggests that the people felt abandoned by the Moon's strange behaviour and practiced many rituals to bring back order to their skies.

The Masai tribes of Africa threw sand in the air, the North American Indians rattled their pots and pans, whilst others fired arrows at the sky to rid the Moon of her predator. In China they banged on mirrors to frighten away the dragon that they believed was eating the Moon. Some rituals for encouraging the return of the Moon however, were far more sinister. In Mexico, dwarves and hunchbacks were sacrificed, whilst dogs and babies were beaten until they howled and cried.

In northern Europe, the lunar eclipse was marked by various means, including shouting, performing magical acts, juggling and chanting whilst divining, all of which was condemned by various Christian sects.

Other cultures thankfully believed in more romantic explanations for the lunar eclipse. Both the Bangala tribe in Africa and the Australian Aborigines, believed that the Sun loved the Moon so much that He was forever chasing Her across the sky, although He could never quite catch Her. During a lunar eclipse however, He finally caught up with Her to indulge in a passionate meeting that was concealed by the resulting darkness.

Whatever measures have, or are, still employed to restore the Moon to Her former golden self, they always work, for the Moon, after a short time, returns to normal. These rituals therefore, like all superstitions, become embedded in the tradition and folklore of their specific culture and continue down the years, albeit somewhat sanitised and regardless of scientific education.

Eclipses, whether lunar or solar, have always been viewed with foreboding by the inhabitants of the Earth, and throughout history, have been a recurring theme in some of our great literary works and sacred texts.

In Shakespeare's Richard 11 (Act 11, Scene iv), an army captain who is waiting for the king states:

> *'The pale-fac'd moon looks bloody on the earth,*
> *And lean-look'd prophets whisper fearful change…*
> *These signs forerun the death or fall of kings.'*

In the biblical book of Acts 2:20, we are told of the words of the prophet Joel concerning the day of Judgement:

'The sun will be turned to darkness and the moon to blood before the coming of the great and glorious day of the Lord.'

Many ancient peoples were well versed in predicting both solar and lunar eclipses. The Mayans, Babylonians, Greeks, Chinese and Egyptians, all had sufficient knowledge to understand that lunar eclipses follow a repetitive cycle of exactly 6585.3 days (approximately eighteen years).

With the invention of the Gutenberg press in the fifteenth century, 'almanacs' (a word derived from Arabic meaning, 'calendar of the skies'), were printed, which gave information on forthcoming celestial events, something that was to prove extremely useful for the famous explorer, Christopher Columbus.

In 1504, Columbus arrived in the West Indies with a ravenous and mutinous crew. Due to a dispute with the natives, a Jamaican chief threatened to withhold food supplies, leaving Columbus in a very precarious position. He had in his possession however, a copy of the published almanac and saw to his relief that on that very evening of March 1st, a lunar eclipse was due to take place.

Columbus therefore warned the Jamaican chief that if he continued to withhold food supplies, he would make the Moon disappear. That evening as darkness fell and the Moon began to gradually turn blood red, the terrified chief relented, and the hungry crew were fed.

In 1964, Professor Gerald Hawkins, an astronomer at Boston University, carried out detailed tests on Stonehenge. These tests followed claims by various archaeologists and astronomers that the ancient monument had been built not only to plot the movement of the Sun and the Moon, but also to help predict both solar and lunar eclipses.

Hawkins eventually concluded that Stonehenge was indeed used to calculate both types of eclipse, in addition to having the ability to measure the tides, and predict perigees (See Chapter 4) to within an accuracy of approximately three hours every fifty years.

A lunar eclipse is therefore a biannual occurrence of nature and although now scientifically understood, it remains an event that still has the power to invoke wonder and a certain amount of consternation, as the sky darkens and the golden orb becomes seemingly engorged with blood.

The Blue Moon

Today, the term 'Blue Moon', refers to the rare event where a second full Moon occurs in the same calendar month, giving rise to the phrase, 'once in a blue Moon' meaning very occasionally.

This meaning, with which many of us are familiar, actually originated from a mistake printed in the Sky and Telescope magazine in 1946. The error was corrected by the magazine some fifty-three years later, but the term had, by that time, become both established and popular in the English language. Hence the phrase, Blue Moon, remains the preferred and popular description for the second of two full Moons occurring in the same calendar month.

A Blue Moon will therefore, occur once every 2.72 years, usually during the months of July, August or October, thus bringing the number of full Moons in a calendar year to thirteen rather than twelve.

An even rarer event than one Blue Moon is when there are two Blue Moons in a year, which only happens approximately every nineteen years in January and March. The predetermining factor in order for this to happen is that February has no full Moon as was the case in 2018.

A much older, and some say the original meaning of the term Blue Moon, was written in the 'Maine Farmer's Almanac' in the early twentieth century. The Almanac stipulated that the four seasons, determined by the position of the Sun, should, in theory, each have three full Moons. Due however, to the slight change in the equinoxes and solstices each solar year, some seasons have four full Moons rather than three, and that it is actually the third full Moon in a season, and not the fourth, which earns the title of the Blue Moon.

The phrase 'Blue Moon' was in use long before it became associated with an extra Moon. In the sixteenth century, referring to the Moon as blue was equivalent to saying it was made of green cheese, and the term came to mean something that was quite absurd. The phrase first appeared in this context in the Oxford English dictionary during that time, where it is referenced to a proverb:

'If they say the moon is blue
We must believe that it is true'

During the nineteenth century, the phrase became altered again both in words and meaning and the phrase, 'until a Blue Moon' came into use, which meant 'never'.

Until 1582, when the Gregorian calendar reforms were made, each full Moon had an ecclesiastical name upon which the Jewish festivals (and Easter) were calculated. The introduction of the revised solar calendar however, dispensed with this system, and it was decided that any extra Moon that occurred during the ecclesiastical year should be referred to as 'blue'. The choice of colour however still remains a mystery.

Finally, the term Blue Moon is also employed when the Moon actually appears to be blue in colour, normally due to atmospheric pollution caused by major volcanic eruptions. Records tell of the Moon appearing blue after the eruption of Krakatoa in 1883.

The term Blue Moon can therefore be said to be somewhat of a misnomer, and is just another of the Silver Lady's anomalies. It is certainly one that conjures up tales of mystery and magick, and carries our imagination to a land of fantasy and dreams.

The Black Moon

The term 'Black Moon' is perhaps not so well known as that of the Blue Moon, although it too has been given various meanings as millennia have passed.

The first theory is that it refers to a month when there is no new Moon, a situation that can only occur in the shortest month of February, and this was probably the origin of the term, referring to the fact that it was a month without new Moon light.

The second explanation is that it refers to a month when there is no full Moon, again an event that can only occur in February.

The third explanation can once more be found in the 'Maine Farmer's Almanac' where the four seasons, determined by the position of the Sun, should, in theory, have three new Moons each. However due to the slight change in the dates of the equinoxes and solstices each solar year, some seasons have four New Moons rather than three, and it is the third Moon in that season and not the fourth that earns the title of the Black Moon.

The final explanation resembles the more modern explanation for the Blue Moon, i.e. it refers to the presence of a second new Moon within the same calendar month, but this never occurs in February as it is simply not long enough.

In the same way as the Blue Moon, the Black Moon is yet another strange phenomenon that occurs every two to three years, and once again causes us to ponder and perhaps become embroiled in strange rituals, regardless of the logic of science.

Other Solar System Moons

Although Earth has only one Moon, there are currently more than a hundred and ninety known Moons in our Solar System. Pictures taken by the Hubble Telescope however, suggest there are many more waiting to be discovered, especially around the outer planets.

Considering the many effects that our Moon has upon the Earth, we can only imagine the influences of numerous Moons that comprise of different sizes and complex materials on the various planets within our Solar System.

Looking at the planets in order of their closeness to the

Sun, we see that the two planets that are nearest, namely Mercury and Venus, do not have any Moons, whilst Earth has just one. Next in line is Mars, which has two Moons, called **Phobos** and **Deimos** (the latter is the smallest Moon in the Solar System).

Jupiter meanwhile, the largest planet in our solar system, currently boasts sixty-seven Moons, the four largest of which are:

- **Callisto:** The outermost of the four, heavily cratered and thought to hold a body of water.

- **Io:** The innermost Moon and the most sulphurous and volcanic, with hundreds of volcanoes erupting at any one time. It also appears to have an atmosphere.

- **Europa:** This has an icy surface that may cover liquid water.

- **Ganymede:** The largest Moon in the Solar System, being larger in diameter than Mercury, with its own magnetic field.

The fascinating planet of Saturn is probably most famous for its spectacular ring system, comprising of ice particles which orbit the planet. There are three main rings (A to C) and several fainter dustier, narrow rings, each of which is separated by gaps known as divisions.

In addition, Saturn also currently has sixty-two named Moons, many of which have quite unique qualities:

- **Titan:** Saturn's largest Moon has a thick, organic-rich nitrogen atmosphere, which may resemble primitive Earth before the dawn of life.

- **Mimas:** This has a huge crater, possibly caused by a meteorite.

- **Enceladus:** This has an exceptionally bright surface, caused by underwater volcanoes.

- **Tethys:** This has a canyon running three quarters of the way round its surface, suggesting that it may once have nearly been split in half.

- **Dione and Rhea:** Both have mysterious white wispy markings.

- **Hyperion:** Probably the strangest Moon as it is a peculiar shape, and the length of its days are constantly changing.

- **Iapetus:** This is a half-light and half dark Moon.

- **Pan:** This is a tiny walnut-shaped Moon (just twelve miles in diameter) and was only discovered in 1990. It sits within the Encke division in Saturn's 'A' ring. This division or gap is named after Johann Encke, a German astronomer, who took a particular interest in observing the rings of Saturn.

Uranus currently has twenty-seven Moons, many of which have mountains standing over ten miles high, resulting in incredibly deep valleys and vast empty plains, with mysterious dark surfaces. Uranus' Moons range from twenty-five to over eleven hundred miles in diameter.

Neptune currently has fourteen Moons, the most well-known of which are **Triton** and **Nereid**, the former having an atmosphere, and a surface comprising of a thin layer of methane and nitrogen over water ice.

Finally, there is Pluto (the now reclassified dwarf planet), which currently has five Moons, the largest of which is **Charon**, and is the Moon closest in size to its associated planet.

No doubt that as more powerful equipment becomes available, astronomers will discover more Moons, each of which will have their own role, regardless of their size. This serves to remind us that no matter how small we may seem in the greater scheme of things, we each have our own unique part to play in the rich tapestry of life.

Mrs Darley Tale: Whosoever Plays the Flute...

It was one of those intoxicating mornings that only fall in mid-summer, when colours are brighter, bird song clearer, and perfumed flowers sweeter.

Discovering that I'd forgotten to buy any butter when I went on my weekly shopping trip the previous evening, I decided to take full advantage of the warm weather and began to walk the mile or so up to the village shop.

I was half-way to my destination, when a white car coming towards me down the single-track lane slowed down as it approached, and through the open window a familiar voice called, 'Good morning'.

'Oh hello, Phyllis,' I said smiling, for I was always

pleased to see her. 'Are you going down to see Mrs D?'

Phyllis nodded. 'Yes, we're going to the fete down in the village hall later. But tell me, where are you off to on foot?'

'Just to the village shop. I forgot to buy butter yesterday and it's such a beautiful day, I felt I just had to walk - almost as though the morning called out to me.'

For the briefest of moments, I thought I saw a frown fleetingly cross Phyllis' face.

'Called out to you in what way?' The frown had gone as quickly as it came, but her question puzzled me.

'Oh, I don't know really. Just a longing to be out in the summer sunshine.'

'You know it's the Blue Moon today, don't you?' She asked.

'Yes, of course.' I was rather surprised that she thought I'd forgotten. 'Aren't we all celebrating together later?'

Her smile seemed a little forced. 'Yes, yes of course we are. Well, enjoy your walk and I'll see you later on.' She wound up her window and drove off down the lane.

I couldn't help but ponder during the remainder of my walk on Phyllis' rather odd comments and behaviour, but eventually managed to push them to the back of my mind, and upon my return from the shop, spent the remainder of the day relaxing in the garden.

***

The Sun had just disappeared behind Sharp Tor when I heard voices outside on the path, and wrapping up warmly, I went to join my neighbours and associated guests in Mrs Darley's garden.

As I opened the gate, it was like stepping into how I imagined the land of the fae might look. Jam jars containing tea lights were secreted into the niches of the dry stonewalls, and just outside the old summerhouse, stood two smoking pot-bellied barbeques, emitting the most mouth-watering aromas.

'This looks wonderful,' I said, eyeing all the delicious food that was sizzling on the griddle.

'Then just tell Bod what you want,' said Mrs Darley, after greeting me with a customary hug. 'He's on cooking duty.'

'Oh my goodness,' I said, taking a plate, 'it all looks so lovely I don't know what to have.'

'Then let me suggest a hot skewer of marinated vegetables and prawns to begin,' said Bod.

'Thank you,' I said, as he lifted the food onto my plate with a pair of tongs. 'I certainly didn't expect anything so elaborate.'

'Well we have to celebrate in style when we have a rare occasion like this. I've always been away at sea whenever there's been a Blue Moon, so I'm looking forward to tonight, after all it will be another two and a half years before the next one.'

'Oh,' I said, impressed that a Blue Moon could be calculated so precisely, 'I didn't realise.'

He grinned. 'That's why the expression, 'once in a Blue Moon' means infrequently.'

I thanked him for both the food and the information and then moved away, for others were already queuing behind me with their plates at the ready. Like Bod, I too was determined to enjoy the unusual evening that lay ahead.

When everyone had taken their fill of food and each guest had a glass of either red wine or whiskey to hand, Mrs Darley sat down in an old deck chair beside the still smouldering barbeque in front of the summerhouse. The rest of us, with the exception of Phyllis who was given the honorary 'comfy chair', sat on blankets that had been spread out on the lawn.

'Well,' said Mrs Darley, smiling at the assembled group before her, 'welcome one and all to our Blue Moon celebrations. This evening brings together those who have experienced these celebrations before, and also a few 'first timers', who are no doubt wondering what the fuss is all about.

'Now, for those of you who are unfamiliar with the stories associated with the Blue Moon, what you are about to hear may alarm you, although it is not meant to do so, and for those of you who are more than familiar with the folk lore of the Blue Moon, a timely reminder that will not go amiss.'

I suddenly shivered, unsure whether this was due to the waning warmth of the dying barbeque or because of what her words implied, and I instinctively pulled my cardigan more closely around my shoulders.

'The Blue Moon, as I'm sure some of you are aware, is a rare event that happens approximately every two and a half years, usually during the months of August, October and, as is the case today, July, when we have two full Moons falling in the same calendar month.'

'Doesn't it have other meanings though?' Asked Don.

Mrs Darley smiled. 'It does indeed, Don, although you'll be pleased to hear that I'm not going to bore you with them all tonight. What I have just described is probably the most popular definition and is one that has managed to accumulate some rather curious folklore.'

My heart began to beat a little faster as it often did when Mrs Darley began her magickal and mystical tales, and I listened with much wonder, some disbelief, and a certain amount of understanding regarding Phyllis' reaction earlier that day.

'There are some souls, so legend would have us believe,

who have become bewitched beneath the Blue Moon and have inadvertently found themselves, shall we say, 'spirited away'.'

'Where to?' Rose and Bod's young daughter Lucy asked eagerly. This was her first Blue Moon celebration too, as it was the first time she had been considered old enough to join in.

'All in good time, my dear, all in good time.' Mrs Darley smiled at her before continuing with her tale.

'It is said, that on Blue Moon days such as these, when the air is clear and warm, the sound of haunting music can often be heard, carried on the breeze to the unsuspecting ear.'

'The music is so beautiful, and so intoxicating, that whoever hears it is compelled to follow wherever it may lead. Eventually, the bewitched person begins to dance in a way they have never danced before. They perform a dance of pure delight, often called the dance of ecstasy.'

'Ooo! I'd love to dance like that.' Rose laughed and winked at Bod.

'Ah no, Rose – no, trust me, you wouldn't,' said Mrs Darley shaking her head, 'for the dance of the Blue Moon is so heady and so intoxicating that afterwards, nothing ever quite compares to it. It is said that many have gone on to suffer from what is termed 'Blue Moon madness', and that they spend their whole lives simply waiting to hear the music again.'

For a moment there was silence as we took in what Mrs Darley had just told us. Then someone laughed.

'A wonderful legend,' said a dark-haired man whom I had not met before, and who seemed to be an acquaintance of Don's. 'But not one that anyone with an iota of sense is going to take seriously. Let's just hope that Don hasn't brought his flute along tonight.'

'Ah, you may mock, John,' said Phyllis, 'but those very pipes are thought to have been heard not too far from here.'

'Is that so?' John murmured, still sounding rather sceptical.

'Phyllis is right', said Eddie, 'that's what they reckon happened to Ellie Botallick's Grandmother up at Penlee Farm over the back of the tor there, albeit many years ago now.' He turned to our host. 'Will you tell the tale, Mrs D?'

'Of course. For it is without doubt, a tale that deserves to be heard. And so my dears,' Mrs Darley settled herself back in her deck chair, 'Alice Botallick was a quiet woman by all accounts, kind and hardworking, and on the morning of a Blue Moon, she went out onto the tor to gather some gorse flowers in order to make her wine. Two hours passed, and when she failed to return home, her husband went out to look for her. He searched and searched, until eventually he found her at the bottom of the tor by the stream.'

Lucy's eyes widened. 'Was she hurt?'

'Fortunately not, my dear. Instead, she was dancing, but dancing in a way he had never seen before, and certainly not by his wife. It was wild, it was erotic, it was (so her husband said), almost as though she was dancing for someone else…a lover perhaps…'

Mrs Darley lapsed into silence for moment as we each allowed this image to play out in our minds eye.

'Eventually, exhausted, Alice Botallick collapsed, and her husband carried her home, where she gradually began to gain consciousness. But…' Mrs Darley leaned forward and raised a warning finger in the air, 'from that day, until the day she died, she simply sat and stared out of the window, never uttering a word, never moving, except…'

We all waited.

'Whenever she heard the sound of the flute, a wistful smile would spread across her face, and she would sway gently in her chair, as though remembering that day she danced on the tor. Her family always maintained that she had been bewitched by the flute on the morning of the Blue Moon.'

We all sat in silence, entranced by Mrs Darley's story, John included.

'Of course, my dears,' said Mrs Darley, 'the sound of the flute has always been associated with magick, and was thought to arouse the imps of lust. As St John Chrysostom, a fourth century Bishop of Constantinople, once said, "Whosoever plays the flute, summons the demons.".'

I sat, both charmed and just a little disturbed by what I had heard. It certainly explained Phyllis's barely concealed concern earlier in the day when I said I had felt 'called' to walk up the lane.

'And here She is.' Don suddenly pointed eastwards towards the horizon where the Moon was beginning to make her ascent above the peaks of Dartmoor.

'Then we must raise our glasses,' said Mrs Darley, as we all made a rather undignified attempt at scrambling to our feet in order to face the Moon.

'Tonight, may we all come to know the beauty and ecstasy of the Blue Moon in our lives, but fail to become bewitched by her. To the Blue Moon.'

'To the Blue Moon.' Our heartfelt toast rang out across the garden, almost as though we were attempting to prevent Her from tempting us with the sensual delights of the Blue Moon flute.

***

Upon leaving the gathering a little while later, Mrs Darley

hurried after me along the path.

'I hope we haven't frightened you tonight with our Blue Moon stories my dear,' she said.

'No, no, of course not. I found it fascinating…a little unnerving, but fascinating.'

'And that's exactly how it should be. Everything upon this Earth has an opposite, a shadow side. Everything of beauty has a thread of ugliness, everything that enchants has the power to possess, and everything that shines also knows the dark.'

'Like the Moon,' I said.

She nodded and smiled. 'Exactly. Like the Moon.'

The following poem was inspired both by Mrs Darley's story of Alice Botallick, coupled with my own fascination with the Goat Foot God, Pan.

The Pipes of Pan

Beneath the Moon
The pure notes dance,
They bewitch and beguile,
Enchant and entrance.

Come child come and follow me,
Drown in honeyed ecstasy.

Let me lead you
Far away,
Beyond the toils
Of everyday.

Come child come and follow me,
Drown in honeyed ecstasy.

Harken, to
The pipes of Pan,
Too strong a lure
For mortal man.

Come child come and follow me
Drown in honeyed ecstasy

Chapter Four

Moon Tides

Mrs Darley Tale: The Release

'Oh good, you're back.' Rose's voice rang out across the hamlet as she came out of her cottage and crossed the narrow lane to greet me.

'Yes, thank goodness,' I said, taking my briefcase and suitcase out of the car. 'That was a long week's course, and driving back from Bristol in the Friday night rush hour isn't my idea of fun.'

'I can imagine,' she said, 'but at least you're home in time to join us later.'

'Join you for what?' I asked, wondering how I could excuse myself from what I assumed would be a late night. I was tired, and all I wanted at that precise moment was a hot bath and a good night's sleep.

Rose pointed towards the five barred gate as it squeaked open. 'Here comes Phyllis and Mrs D – you can ask them.'

'Hello dear,' Mrs Darley walked up onto the lane and greeted me with a hug. 'How lovely to see you back safe and sound. Did you have a good week?'

I nodded. 'Tiring, but informative.'

'That's no excuse though, is it Mrs D?' Asked Rose.

'No excuse for what?'

'Not joining us tonight.'

There was, I thought, a rather sudden and awkward silence, and I became aware of the disapproving look that Mrs Darley directed at Rose.

'I don't think Carole was trying to make an excuse at all,' said Phyllis, making a diplomatic attempt at filling the silence. 'I'm sure she's tired after her week away and will just want to sit and put her feet up.'

'Quite,' agreed Mrs Darley.

I meanwhile, was feeling quite perplexed and embarrassed by the whole conversation. Clearly something was happening tonight that Mrs Darley wished to keep secret.

Rose however, oblivious to her *faux pas*, continued on regardless. 'Still, going in the sea will do her a power of good, especially after being cooped up all week.'

I looked at Rose. 'Going in the sea...*tonight*?'

'It's an Equinox tradition,' said Rose, 'well, as long as the weather, the Moon and the tides are right. And tonight they are.'

'Right for what?' I asked.

She laughed. 'To perform a little bit of Moon water magick of course.'

I looked at her, feeling rather bewildered. There it was again, that unnerving word, *magick*...

***

Eddie's old minibus swung round onto the narrow harbour just as dusk was beginning to creep across the sea, colouring it deep violet against the sky's last pale pink threads of daylight.

Everyone scrambled out of the van, and within a few minutes, we were all standing on the edge of the harbour, allowing the breeze to toy with our hair, tasting the salt of the sea, and listening to the breaking waves, soft and gentle upon the sand of the sheltered cove.

'Oh,' said Rose, suddenly pointing over the harbour wall,

'here comes the Moon. Come on everybody.'

I watched, as everyone began to strip down to their swimwear before throwing their clothes rather unceremoniously in the back of the van.

'Aren't you joining us?' Peter asked, as I remained fully clothed beside the van.

'I er...' I began.

'Of course she is,' said Rose.

Feeling somewhat under pressure and too embarrassed to admit the fact that I was a poor swimmer, I threw my clothes on top of those already in the van and was soon standing, dressed for the sea, shivering in the moonlight.

Within a few minutes, we were making our way down the rough granite steps that led onto the sandy beach of the small cove.

'What time is it, Eddie dear?' Aasked Mrs Darley, who had remained uncharacteristically quiet up until now. 'You're the only person with a waterproof watch.'

'Just after half seven.'

'Well, the tide's on the turn, so we'd better take the plunge,' said Peter laughing, as we all let out a collective groan at his dreadful pun.

Rose, Peter, Eddie, Mrs Darley and much to my surprise, Phyllis, all joined hands and began to walk in a line rather gingerly towards the now darkened water's edge, where the waves tumbled onto the sand.

'Come on,' said Phyllis gently, turning back towards me and holding out her hand as though sensing my hesitation.

I managed to find a smile from somewhere and reluctantly took her hand.

The shock of the cold water, despite the warmth of the day, made me gasp, and I began to panic. How much further would we wade out before I was out of my depth? I had never been fond of the water and always made sure my toes could make contact with the bottom of a pool or the sea-bed. Now, in the dark, and with the water up to my waist, I was seriously out of my comfort zone.

Mrs Darley's voice suddenly broke into my thoughts. 'I think this will do. We're in quite deep enough for our purposes.'

In that moment I could have hugged her, and whatever the evening was about to hold, at least I would still be able to feel the sand beneath my feet.

'Let us make a circle,' said Mrs Darley. 'Peter, Eddie and Bod, you can all go out where it's a little deeper, and leave us shorter folk in shallower waters.'

With our circle formed, and light of the waning gibbous Moon making the sea shine like obsidian glass, we stood as a reflected image in a scrying mirror.

'Who's going first?' Asked Rose, the excitement evident in her voice.

'Well, my dear,' said Mrs Darley, 'before we get started, I think it would only be polite to offer our newcomer here an explanation of what we are about to do.'

'Oh yes, sorry,' said Rose, turning to me. 'Well, the whole point is that we're going to wash away things like fears and negative thoughts.'

'Oh,' I said as the fear of being out of my depth threatened to return.

'It's something we try and do once a year,' said Phyllis, 'whenever the natural world is in alignment with what we're trying to achieve.'

I remained silent, not quite sure I understood what she meant.

Mrs Darley must have sensed my uncertainty. 'What they're trying to tell you, is that we are about to perform a simple act of magick, whilst utilising the energies of nature. At this precise moment, the tide is beginning to ebb, the

Moon is in its waning phase and today is the autumn equinox, a time when the balance tips, and the energies encourage us to let go of things which no longer serve our highest and greatest good.'

'Oh, I see,' I said, as suddenly this ceremony about washing away fears and negative thoughts began to make more sense.

'So,' said Rose, 'all you have to do is focus on what no longer belongs in your life, and when it's your turn, simply imagine letting it go.'

I nodded, not liking to ask what she meant by 'your turn'. My turn to do what exactly?

'Shall we make a start?' Rose asked eagerly. 'I'm happy to go first.'

'Then go ahead, dear,' said Mrs Darley.

I watched as Rose released the hands of those either side of her and bobbed into our midst, whilst our circle closed around her. Then, in a beautiful clear voice Mrs Darley began to chant.

'Now beneath this waning moon,
No longer is it time to hide,
Fears and worries, stress and woes
Release them now on ebbing tide.'

Phyllis then joined in the second round of the chant and finally the rich voices of Peter, Eddie, and Bod, swelled the chorus of sound, as the Sea Gods lifted our bodies gently with each ebbing wave.

Suddenly, Rose took a deep breath, and within an instant disappeared beneath the waves.

Seconds later she reappeared, her body glistening and her eyes sparkling in the moonlight, as though she had been cleansed of everything in the world that had weighed her down.

I watched as Phyllis, Peter, Bod, and Eddie each took their turn. I could feel my heart begin to pound as I knew Mrs Darley would insist that I went before her. The thought of going under the water filled me with terror, and I desperately tried to think of an excuse not to partake in this tidal baptism.

All too soon however, Phyllis and Eddie released my hands, and I found myself gently guided into the centre of the circle.

'Whenever you're ready dear,' said Mrs Darley, as she and the others began the chant.

> *'Now beneath this waning moon,*
> *No longer is it time to hide,*
> *Fears and worries, stress and woes*
> *Release them now on ebbing tide.'*

I knew that I couldn't back out now, but suddenly, as the chant rose to a crescendo, I no longer wanted to. I realised that I *was* full of fear. Fear of a past relationship, fear of failure, fear of not being good enough, fear of rejection, and fear of going under water. In that moment, I decided that if my fear of water could be overcome, then perhaps the other fears that so often constricted certain areas of my life could also be washed away. I took a deep breath, sank below the surface, and allowed the black sea to envelop me.

I reappeared a few seconds later, somewhat less dignified and with a certain amount of spluttering, but nevertheless I had done it. On that equinox ebbing tide, beneath the light of the waning gibbous Moon, I had finally begun to release my fears into the arms of the sea gods.

Call of the Moon Tides

The beauty of our Moon in Her full glory can never be denied, but little thought, if any, is given to the power that hides behind that captivating face. She can be outwardly forceful, as evidenced by Her control of our tidal waters, weather patterns and earth tides, but She can also be quietly influential, as experienced by many who behave and feel differently beneath Her full light, all of which only adds to Her mysterious qualities.

Yet, how can a satellite that orbits our planet some 238,000 miles away, exert such power over our lives? This question is one that has been debated for centuries by scientists, astronomers, astrologers and those who have simply experienced Her potency as the month rolls by.

The Highs and Lows of Tidal Waters

The oceanic tides are caused by the varying strength of the Moon's gravitational pull at different points on the Earth, known as bulges and depressions. When the Earth passes beneath a bulge (approximately every twelve hours and twenty-five minutes), our tidal waters are subject to a high tide, and although we experience on average two high tides per day, they do in fact, occur for different reasons, albeit the Moon is responsible for both.

The oceans on the side of the Earth nearest to the Moon are subject to the power of its pull, and despite the force of inertia (that which attempts to keep things in balance), exerted by the Earth, it is unable to compete with the power of the Moon's magnetic force, therefore causing a swelling of the water which we refer to as a high tide.

At the same time, the waters on the opposite side of the Earth, i.e. furthest away from the Moon, also experience a high tide, but this time it *is* due to the force of inertia. In this instance, the pull of the Moon on the side of the Earth closest to the Moon is stronger than the Moon's pull on the waters on the opposite side of the Earth, and as the Earth moves slightly towards the Moon, this causes the waters furthest away from the Moon to bulge.

Meanwhile, at an angle of ninety degrees between the two bulges, the Earth and its waters pass through a depression, and at these points two low tides occur.

Spring and Neap Tides

Twice monthly, these tidal effects are enhanced when, not only is the Earth subject to the gravitational pull of the Moon, but also to that of the Sun, as they align at both the full and new Moons. At these times, the high tides are greater than normal, and are referred to as 'spring tides'.

Meanwhile at the waxing and waning quarter moon phases, the weakest or lowest tides occur, and are referred to as 'neap tides'.

Perigee and Apogee

In the second century BCE, the Greek astronomer, Hipparchus, observed that the Moon's orbit around the Earth was not a perfect circle, and that the Moon wandered slightly in towards the Earth, and then out again, rather as though it were attached by a fixed spring.

When the Moon is at its furthest point from Earth, it is known as being in *apogee,* deriving from the Greek words *apo* meaning away and *gaia* or *gē* meaning 'Earth'. When the Moon is at its closest point to Earth it is referred to as being in *perigee,* from the Greek word *peri* meaning 'near', and again, *gaia* or *gē* meaning 'Earth'.

Although most of us would not be able to notice a difference in size when looking at a full Moon in perigee against seeing it in apogee, it *is* noticeably brighter when in perigee due to the fact it is approximately 31,200 miles closer to Earth.

This was a fact that NASA had to take into account during the planning of the successful Apollo 11 mission of 21st July 1969, when Neil Armstrong and Buzz Aldrin first walked on the Moon. At that time, the Moon was approaching the greatest perigee of that year, meaning that not only did the astronauts have to travel thousands of miles less than they would have done at any other time that year, but a huge amount of fuel was also saved.

The apogee and perigee also cause the Moon to vary in speed. It is at its slowest at the apogee and its fastest at the perigee, albeit the differing lunar phases, the declination cycle (the angle of the Moon's orbit) and the pull of the Sun also effect its overall speed.

Unsurprisingly, when the Moon comes closest to Earth at the perigee, the tides are strongly influenced, and when this coincides with a full or new Moon, the effects are enhanced even further, often producing either such high tides that coastal flooding occurs, or such low tides that areas of land are exposed which are normally under water, such as ancient petrified forests.

Tide Waves or 'Bores'

Tide waves or 'bores' (from the Scandinavian word *bara*, meaning wave, swell or billow), naturally appear throughout the world in rivers with large tidal ranges.

A bore forms when the tide rises in a narrowing channel into the shape of a funnel. Dependant on wind speed, this funnel of water can travel at an average speed of sixteen kilometres per hour, and has been known to reach two metres in height.

Bores can occur when the Sun aligns with the Moon and the Earth at the full and new Moons, resulting in high spring tides, although they may not be particularly impressive. When the Sun is directly over the equator at the spring and autumn equinoxes (around 21st March and 21st September respectively) however, this is when the highest tides occur, especially if the Moon is also in perigee and it is at these times that the largest bores can be seen.

The Severn estuary in Bristol has the second highest tidal range in the world, with the difference between the highest and lowest tide in any one day being more than 14.5 metres. It is here, along the lower reaches of the River Severn in Gloucestershire, that some of the most spectacular bores in the world can be seen.

Not only are the bores impressive in size, but the strange phenomenon of the river actually flowing the wrong way for up to an hour after the bore has passed is quite a spectacle to witness. Eventually, the river appears to stand still for a while until it reverts back to its normal direction of flow. In 1824, Thomas Harrel observed the Severn bore as follows:

'When the bore comes, the stream does not swell by degrees, as at other times, but rolls in with a head foaming and roaring, as though it were enraged by the opposition it encounters.'

The River Trent also has a similar phenomenon, although its tidal wave is not referred to as a bore, but rather an *aegir*, named after the Norse God of the seashore or ocean.

Just as Nordic sailors feared their God Aegir, so those who lived on the banks of the River Trent also feared the Trent *aegir*, due to its unpredictability. It was renowned for its fury, and was often strong enough to destroy or damage ships and boats as it passed. In times past, when small craft were moored on the river, it was customary to shout 'Ware Eagre!' to warn of its approach. *Aegir* may also derive from the Old English *ēagor*, meaning a flood or body of water.

In 1013, the Viking King, Svein Forkbeard along with his son, Canute, arrived with an army to conquer England, and moored his ships in the haven at Morton Bight, near Gainsborough on the River Trent. A year after Svein's death, Canute became King and is famously remembered for turning back the tide. Some believe this occurred on the seashore, whilst others claim it refers to the turn of the *aegir* on the River Trent.

Just as with the Severn bore, the *aegir* is visible during the twice-monthly spring tides although again, the spring and autumn equinoxes are recommended for observing the most spectacular *aegirs*.

Earthquakes and Volcanoes

If the Moon can exert sufficient pull on the Earth to move it, and as a result, affect the oceanic tides, then we must consider its effect on the Earth with regards to other natural phenomenon, such as earthquakes and volcanoes. It may be possible that as the Moon makes its monthly orbit around the Earth, weaknesses in the Earth's surface become more and more stressed, especially when the magnetic pull is stronger at the full or new Moon, or when the Moon is in apogee or perigee.

The Moon experiences approximately three thousand quakes per annum, and the frequency of these increases when the Moon's orbit brings it closer to the Earth. It seems likely therefore that a similar phenomenon should occur here on Earth.

The Earth is made up of tectonic plates that float over a molten mass, each of which are moved around by the gravitational pull of the Moon. Occasionally these plates become dislodged sufficiently for a natural disaster to occur.

That is not to say that every time the Moon is new, full, in perigee, or apogee that some major disaster will take place. It is thought that the Moon must pass over a weak point in the surface of the Earth many times before the fault gives way, resulting in an earthquake or volcanic eruption.

In 1980, G. A. Eilby wrote a book entitled *Earthquakes*, in which he listed all the earthquakes that had occurred around the world since 1505. Of these, ninety-six percent occurred either on, or within one day of either a new or full Moon, or the Moon being in apogee or perigee, whilst seventy-five percent occurred when two of these extreme events happened on the same day.

Atmospheric Tides

The Earth's atmosphere is vital to the survival of life on this planet, and consists of various gases including nitrogen and oxygen, which make up what we refer to as 'air'. The roles of our atmosphere are many and varied and offer protection against:

- The extreme heat and cold of space.
- The harmful radiation rays of the Sun.
- Millions of small meteors, which are burned up before they can damage the Earth.
- Drought, as water is drawn up from the world's oceans and recycled as rain.

Weather patterns are therefore, simply a result of the Moon pulling the atmosphere around, a discovery made by two British scientists, Appleton and Weeks, in 1939. Wherever the Moon happens to be in relation to the Earth, the weather will be affected in some way.

Many studies have shown that specific weather patterns occur during various phases of the Moon, although there are many other contributory factors that all play a major part in determining the weather and can include:

- Whether the Moon is in apogee or perigee and in which hemisphere these events happen to occur.
- Which other planets happen to be in alignment.
- The presence of sunspots (caused by temporary areas of reduced surface temperature on the Sun).
- In which hemisphere the full Moon occurs During our winter in the northern hemisphere. the full Moon is in the north, whilst during our summer the full Moon is in the south. The opposite occurs at the new Moon.
- The particular weather pattern we are currently in, due to the fact that the Moon behaves rather like a tilting roller coaster, coming back to its start point every 18.6 years. This is known as the 'declination cycle', a fact recognised by the Babylonians.
- The effects of global warming.

Predicting the weather simply by knowing the Moon phase, cannot therefore be guaranteed, but can provide us with an overview of likely trends.

Moon Phase	General Weather Predictions
New Moon **Rises at Dusk** **Sets at Dawn**	Clear mornings. Possible cloudiness at midday (although the Moon in perigee would mean cloudy and rain). Clear and cool at night. Night-time winds at the perigee. If the weather is unsettled, then rain will occur between dusk and dawn.
First Quarter **Rises at Noon** **Sets at Midnight**	Normally settled. Rain before seven, dry by eleven. Thunder after midnight. At perigee, hurricanes are possible. Summer mornings are clear with dew. Winter mornings are cold with frost and snow. Night fog in autumn.
Full Moon **Rises at Sunset** **Sets at Sunrise**	Thunder up to two days after full Moon. Tornadoes possible up to last quarter. Daytime cloud and rain, clearing in the evening (this often continues until the last quarter phase begins). Heat waves in summer. Snow storms in winter. Perigee and apogee result in unusually warm weather.
Last Quarter **Rises at Midnight** **Sets at Noon**	Thunderstorms more possible now than at any other time Cloudy afternoons and evenings with possible evening rain. Dry nights and mornings. Summer very hot. Winter very cold with harsh frosts. Hail.

There are a few old adages that are worth noting when planning an important outdoor event:

- If the Moon is in the sky, there is less likelihood of rain.

- A halo around the Moon means rain.

- A clear Moon heralds a frost in the winter (hence the saying, *'Clear Moon, frost soon'*), or good weather in the summer.

- If the Moon has a reddish or golden tone then rain, wind, or snow is promised.

- Two full Moons in a month will bring a flood.

- *'Pale Moon doth rain,*
  Red Moon doth blow,
  White Moon doth neither
  Rain nor snow.'

- *'If the Moon shows like a silver shield.*
  You need not be afraid to reap your field
  But if she rises haloed round,
  Soon we'll tread on deluged ground.'
                          (Scottish saying)

- *'A fog and a small Moon*
  Bring an easterly wind soon.'
                          (Cornish saying)

- A large star or planet in close proximity to the Moon is said to be a bad weather omen.

- When the old Moon can be seen within the arms of the new Moon, fine weather will follow.

- When the horns of the new Moon turn upward to form a cup, fine weather is forecast, as it is thought that the cupped crescent holds the water and prevents it from falling like rain. This is often referred to as a 'dry Moon.'

- When the new Moon crescent is more upright, rain is likely to fall.

- However, many days old the Moon is on Michaelmas Day (29th September), floods will follow for the same amount of days.

- If Christmas falls during a waxing Moon, the weather will be fair for the following year, but if it falls during a waning Moon then the year will be hard.

- *'Two full Moons in May*
  Neither good for corn nor hay'.
  				(Cornish saying)

Human Tides

Many recognise that the Moon affects us all on both on a physical and psychological level, although the majority of us remain blissfully unaware of the lunar influence on our lives. After all, if the Moon can affect the waters, the Earth and the air, then why should mankind, and indeed all creatures that walk the Earth, escape Her effects?

Anatomically, human beings comprise of between eighty to ninety percent of water, and could therefore, be subject to the magnetic pull of the Moon as She orbits the Earth. In 1962, Dr L J Ravitz suggested in his book, *History, measurement, and applicability of periodic changes in the electromagnetic field in health and disease,* that alterations in human physiology and behaviour could indeed be due to the Moon's influence, albeit not to the body directly, but rather to changes caused in the subtle energy field or aura that surrounds every living thing.

A further possibility is that the Moon exerts Her influence on the intracellular fluid found in the hypothalamus gland. The hypothalamus is the master gland, and as such, controls other various glands situated in the brain. When these glands become stimulated, they release specific neurochemicals into the blood stream which, in turn, affects our moods and emotions.

Menstruation

Women have always had an affinity with the Moon due to the fact that the menstrual cycle mirrors the lunar phase of approximately twenty-eight days. In many languages, the words for Moon, month and menstruation are either identical, or a close derivation of each other.

In cultures where the Moon was seen as feminine, the Moon's phases of new to full and full to dark were mirrored by menstruation, conception and childbirth. Native American legends tell of an umbilical cord, which runs from the Moon to each woman, just like the cord that runs between a Mother and her baby.

In cultures where the Moon was seen as a masculine force, it was still held responsible for menstruation, since it was thought to enter the body of a young woman, either as a god, serpent, bull, or moonbeam, and bring forth a young woman's first period. The Uaupe Indians of the Amazon refer to a pubescent girl's first period as 'defloration by the Moon'.

The first menstrual blood of a young woman was often regarded as magickal, and Pliny, in his *Natural History*, tells us that the witches of Thessaly in Greece collected this treasure, which they named 'Moon-dew', for use in their magickal rituals during a lunar eclipse.

The Maoris considered the Moon to be the 'true husband of all women', because they observed that many of the tribal women menstruated at the time of the dark Moon, or when the new Moon appeared. Menstruation was therefore considered to be the waning of the woman's own Moon.

Our female ancestors were acutely aware of the Moon's cycle, and often found their menstrual cycle to be in synch with the Moon's phases. Today, many women ovulate at the full Moon, when the orb resembles an egg and menstruate at the dark Moon, as this cycle is linked with the desire to procreate.

Other women may experience the opposite cycle where they ovulate at the dark Moon, and menstruate at the full Moon, often referred to as the 'wise woman's cycle'. This cycle occurs more frequently when perhaps the need to mother children has diminished, and a woman's desires turn to creative pursuits and self-expression.

Generally however, our western society has lost touch with the Moon and Her phases and as a result, more and more women are experiencing irregular periods or conception difficulties. It is important to note that in the first instance, medical advice should be always sought if such problems occur.

In 1967, a US physicist called Edmond Dewan, considered the idea that the Moon could have a marked effect on the regularity of a woman's menstrual cycle. He arranged to conduct an experiment on women volunteers who experienced irregular periods. Fourteen days after their last period, he asked the women to leave their bedroom light on all night for three consecutive nights, as this would emulate the full Moon. The experiment's findings strongly suggested that most of the women who took part in the study, began to once again experience a regular menstrual cycle.

In many cultures, the waning of the Moon was a time to be feared, and therefore menstruating women were also looked upon in the same light. They were regarded as both unclean, yet powerful, and some, such as the women of the Dogon tribe in Africa, were banished from the company of the tribe to spend their menstrual days alone.

Again, the Roman writer Pliny, in his *Natural History*, had much to say on the subject:

'Her touch can blast vines, ivy and rue, dry up seeds, make fruit fall off the trees, fade purple cloth, blacken linen in the washtub, tarnish copper, make bees desert their hives and cause abortions in mares, but she can also rid a field of pests by walking round it naked before sunrise, calm a storm at sea by exposing her genitals, and cure boils, hydrophobia and barrenness.'

The biblical text of Leviticus 12:2 tell us:

'A woman who becomes pregnant and gives birth to a son will be ceremoniously unclean for seven days just as she is unclean during her monthly period.'

Even today, in our so-called 'enlightened times', we do little to revere the potent creative power present in all women. Instead, we refer to our periods as 'the curse', or grumble that it is again 'that time of the month', and often see this beautiful monthly occurrence as an inconvenience, rather than the true gift it is.

Marriage and Conception

Not only was the Moon considered responsible for menstruation, it was also thought to be responsible for conception. Following their marriage, Native American women would stand over a pail of water that had been standing in the moonlight, in the belief this would help them conceive. In Europe, married women drank from a water source which had held the reflection of the full Moon.

In countries as far apart as Australia and Greenland, worried parents drew the curtains in their daughters' bedrooms for fear of them becoming pregnant during the three nights of the full Moon.

Even Shakespeare, in his play *Hamlet*, has Laertes warning Ophelia about the potency of the Moon:

> *'The chariest maid is prodigal enough*
> *If she unmask her beauty to the moon.'*

In Brittany, women would cover their bodies to prevent the Moon from impregnating them, especially when the Moon's horns were prominent during the waxing and waning crescents, as they were afraid of being 'Mooned' (French equivalent is *lunée*) and giving birth to a 'Moon-calf' or lunatic child. The horned Moon has long been acknowledged as a symbol of sexual potency, and is often referred to as 'the bull'. In George Stanley Faber's classic book of 1816: *The Origin of Pagan Idolatry: Volume 2 of 3*, he quotes *'A Prayer to the Parasees Invocation of The Moon'*, which begins:

'I adore Ormzud; I adore the Amschaspands; I adore the Moon which preserves the seed of the bull. I adore looking on high; I adore looking below. May the Moon be favourable to me, she who preserveth the seed of the bull.'

In more modern times, Curtis Jackson of the Californian Methodist Hospital, claimed that more babies were conceived during the full Moon, thus supporting the belief that sexual activity increases when the Moon is full.

Although the Moon has often been depicted as the male pursuer of the innocent female, there is one story that reverses this trend and involves the seduction of the Greek Moon Goddess, Selene, by the earthy and lustful Goat Foot God, Pan.

Knowing that the beautiful Selene would never give Herself willingly to him, Pan disguised himself as a ram, and drew Selene into the forest where his lust for Her was sated. Retribution however was swift, as the other deities instantly banished him to the lonely mountains of Arcadia. There he was destined to wander alone for many years, and was said to have amused himself by frightening the occasional traveller, causing them to literally *pan-ic*, which explains the derivation of the word. Pan finally redeemed himself however, as the saviour of the Athenians at the time of the Persian war, and was reinstated as a cult God throughout Greece.

Robert Browning describes this seduction in his poem, 'Pan and Luna'.

*'So lay this Maid-Moon clasped around and caught
By rough red Pan, the God of all that tract.
He it was schemed the snare thus subtly wrought
With simulated earth breath-wool tufts packed
Into a billowy wrappage.'*

In ancient India, the Moon God, Soma, was referred to as the 'first husband of women', and the Rig Veda instructs the bridegroom to say to his bride during the wedding ceremony:

'Soma has acquired thee as his wife'.

In Orkney, marriages always took place under a waxing Moon, with some couples also ensuring the simultaneous rising of the tide, whilst the ancient Greeks preferred the day of the full Moon for their wedding ceremonies.

Childbirth

The Moon, perhaps unsurprisingly, also became inextricably linked with childbirth, and many Moon deities also became patrons of childbirth, regardless of whether they were male or female.

The Sumerian Moon Goddess, Inanna, was referred to as the 'opener of the womb of all women', and Sumerian women would go to Her temple to give birth under the Goddess' protection.

In nineteenth century Ireland, Ulster midwives chanted to the mother-to-be, a song called, *The Moon of the Four Quarters,* whilst placing the cross of St Bride (Bridget) in each of the cardinal points.

'Four corners to her bed.
Four angels at her head.
Mark, Matthew, Luke and John;
God bless the bed that she lies on.
New Moon, new Moon, God bless me.
God bless this house and family.'

Plutarch stated that the full Moon assists childbirth, as it releases more moisture, thereby easing pain. In the past, many women referred to the full Moon as 'the moistener', or 'the dew bringer'. In addition to the full Moon allegedly easing a mother's labour, any child born at the full Moon was said to have a lucky life before him.

In Cornwall it is believed that when a child is born during the waning Moon, the parents' next child will be of the opposite sex. If a child is born during the waxing Moon, then their next child will be of the same sex.

A Cornish saying that remained popular until the 1920's was, *'No Moon, no man'*. This did not necessarily mean death before adulthood, but simply that a child born at the time of the dark Moon would not be particularly robust. This is well illustrated in Hardy's, *'Return of the Native'*:

'No moon, no man. 'Tis one of the truest sayings ever spit out. The boy never comes to anything that's born at the new moon.'

Research carried out by US doctors, Walter and Abraham Menaker, during the 1960's, showed that more babies were born during the three days of the full Moon than at any other time, whilst the fewest births occurred at the new Moon. A German researcher called James W. Buehler, claimed there are many more male births at the full Moon than females.

Death

If the Moon can have such a profound effect on our arrival into this world, why should it not have some influence over our death?

For those who live close to the sea, the tides have always been synonymous with the bringing in and the taking away of life. It is said that a birth will happen on a rising tide and death on an ebbing tide, as mentioned by Charles Dickens in *David Copperfield*, during the death of Barkis:

'People can't die, along the coast', said Mr Peggotty, 'except when the tide's pretty nigh out. They can't be born, unless it's pretty nigh in – not properly born, till flood. He's a-going out with the tide. It's ebb at half-arter three, slack water half-an-hour. If he lives till it turns, he'll hold his own till past the flood, and go out with the next tide.'

General Health

In times past, a person's disposition was categorised into four distinct groups:

- Sanguine (cheerful, confident, optimistic)
- Choleric (bad tempered)
- Phlegmatic (calm and placid)
- Melancholic (depressed or sad)

It was thought that when a person became ill, they should be 'bled' (using leeches), according to an analysis of their disposition at various phases of the Moon's cycle, in order to restore good health.

The sanguine were bled during the first quarter, due to conditions being warm and damp, the choleric were bled between the first quarter and the full Moon, when conditions were warm and dry, the phlegmatic were bled between the full Moon and the last quarter, when conditions were cold and moist, and the melancholic were bled following the last quarter, when conditions were cold and dry.

In more recent times, studies carried out at various hospitals have illustrated how the full Moon has a marked effect upon the outcome of both operations and the increased need for medical treatment.

At the full Moon there are more reports of heart attacks, epilepsy, bladder problems, asthma attacks, gout, and cases of haemorrhaging on the operating table.

Dr Edson J. Andrews, an American Ear, Nose and Throat surgeon, discovered during a study that there was a marked increase in the number of his patients who needed emergency operations around the time of the full Moon. In addition, he said that bleeding increased by up to eighty-two percent following major surgery performed during this Moon phase.

When the full Moon is coupled with being at the perigee, the effects can be quite catastrophic. At the time of both the full Moon and the perigee on June 24th 1994, a tremendous thunderstorm occurred over London, with over fifty more ground strikes of lightning recorded than in an average thunderstorm.

During the following thirty hours, ten times as many people than normal, presented at hospital and GP's surgeries complaining of breathing problems. Over fifty percent of these had never suffered from asthma before. The hospitals were full and began to run out of inhalers, drugs, and staff to cope with the demand.

In contrast however, the Moon is also accredited with healing powers, albeit they may belong to the realms of folklore. In Staffordshire, it was once believed that to cure a child of whooping cough, they should be taken outside and shown the new Moon, after which the mother should lift up the child's clothes, rub her right hand up and down on the child's stomach, and say whilst looking at the Moon's face:

'What I see may it increase;
What I feel may it decrease.'

In Sussex, it was once believed that lymphatic tuberculosis could be cured by lying beneath the new Moon of May, whilst in Devon, it was thought that if corns were cut whilst the Moon was waning, they would gradually disappear.

Moon Madness

We cannot ignore the effect the Moon has on mankind, without exploring certain behavioural changes that have been attributed to the Moon when in its full phase, although such claims are controversial and by no means universally accepted.

Some researchers have stated that at the full Moon there are more cases of:

- Disturbed minds or 'Moon madness'
- Domestic disputes
- Murders and assaults
- Suicides
- Arson
- Violence
- Accidents

- Animal bites
- Aggressive drunkenness
- Road rage
- Burglaries
- People borrowing books from public libraries (perhaps this now translates into eBook purchases?)
- Alcohol consumption (up to a twenty five percent increase)
- Food consumption (up to an eight percent increase)

The first of these, Moon madness, is something which has become embedded within the human psyche, and although many scientists will deny its existence, it has been recognised by various cultures for thousands of years.

The Greek word for madness was *mania,* which derives from the Sanskrit word *ma,* meaning Moon, from which the word, 'maniac' derives. The term 'lunatic' meanwhile, comes directly from the Roman Moon goddess Luna, and the Latin word *tic,* meaning 'struck'.

The British Lunacy Act of 1842 defined a lunatic as:

'A demented person with lucid intervals during the first two phases of the Moon and afflicted with a period of fatuity in the period following after the full Moon.'

Sir Francis Bacon, a sixteenth century English philosopher and statesman stated:

'It is like that the brain of man waxeth moister and fuller upon the full of the Moon'.

This quote, presumably refers to the fact that during the full Moon the brain supposedly becomes less reliable, a fact echoed in Rowley's *The Witch of Edmonton* in 1658, with the line,

'When the Moon's in the full, the wit's in the wane.'

The seventeenth century British physician and medical biographer, Sir William Hale stated:

'The Moon has great influence on all diseases of the brain especially dementia.'

This belief has been reaffirmed in more recent times, due to the research of Doctor Alan M. Beck of Purdue University in the USA. He conducted a longitudinal study of the influence of the Moon on the intensity of behaviours in persons with Alzheimer's disease, including wandering, anxiety, physical aggression and verbal confrontation. His study concluded that persons with Alzheimer's

'…did exhibit significantly more behaviors during periods of full moon.'

In Iceland, it was believed that if a pregnant woman sat and stared at the Moon, her child would be born a lunatic.

The inception of this belief that lunacy was Moon-inspired, was rooted in fear. In the fifteenth century, during the horrific witch-hunts of the Middle Ages, Heinrich Kramer and Jacob Sprenger wrote their infamous 1496 book, the *Malleus Maleficarum ('The Hammer of Witches')*, in which they stated:

'Certain men who are called Lunatics are molested by devils more at one time than another.'

For the inmates of psychiatric hospitals, the full Moon was not an auspicious time. It was thought that many patients were affected by the Moon, therefore leading the staff to give everyone a cautionary whipping in order to temper their behaviour. This of course, proved little comfort to those who also felt the full force of the lunar power. Even today there are more admissions into mental institutions at the full Moon than at any other time.

It therefore stands to reason, that emotions will run particularly high when the full Moon coincides with the perigee, something Shakespeare recognised in his play, *Othello*. When Othello hears of Rodrigo's death he declares:

> *'It is the very error of the Moon,*
> *She comes more near the earth than she was wont,*
> *And makes men mad.'*

Crime figures are also said to rise at the time of the full Moon as many police forces will testify, and Moon-madness has been cited as a defence in several murder trials. Some forces have, in the past, taken the precaution of having more staff on duty at the full Moon, including the Brighton constabulary.

In the 1990's, Christopher Gore, a gifted maths student from Gloucestershire, murdered his parents with an axe whilst the full Moon hung in the sky. He was later questioned about two other murders, which again had occurred at the full Moon. Found guilty, he was given an indefinite sentence in Broadmoor.

During a three-month study of 1,200 inmates in a Yorkshire jail, results showed a huge rise in violence during the days either side of the full Moon.

It seems that mankind has always been more prone to fighting when the Moon is full. Some people attribute this fact to the gravitational pull of the Moon producing a micro storm within the brain, thus increasing adrenalin and testosterone levels.

Even the Allied Invasion of Normandy occurred on the day of the full Moon and the week when the Moon was also in perigee. The weather on June 6th 1944 was stormy, with rough seas and overcast skies, resulting in the Germans being caught off guard in thinking that the inclement weather would prevent any kind of invasion.

Conversely, others believe that the gravitational effects of the Moon are far too miniscule to have any effect on brain activity, and that the Moon is only capable of affecting large open bodies of water rather than the relatively small amount contained within the human body. They also state that any effect that the Moon might have would be the same regardless of the Moon phase, as the Moon is always present, regardless of whether we can see it or not.

Zodiacal Influences

During the twenty-nine-and-a-half days it takes the Moon to travel around the Earth and realign itself with the Sun, it also passes through every sign of the zodiac, spending approximately two and a half days in each.

These short-lived lunar visitations around the constellations, exert various influences upon the Earth, her inhabitants, and the natural world, including horticulture (see Chapter 5).

Astrological Sign of the Moon	Resulting Effects and Influences
Aries	Restlessness can manifest when the Moon is in Aries, although on a positive note, it is a time for new beginnings and ventures.
Taurus	The Taurean Moon may make us feel earthy, sensual and sexual, as this is the sign associated with physical love.
Gemini	The Moon in Gemini often finds us misplacing objects of importance, but it is a good time for travel, buying, selling, communication and learning.
Cancer	This is a time for enjoying home life and its comforts, along with family togetherness, including eating, cooking, gardening, talking and listening to each other. It is also a time when psychic abilities may be heightened.
Leo	Leo is the fire sign of fun and indicates that love, partying, dating, creativity and leisure pursuits of all kinds should be enjoyed. It is also an auspicious time for buying and selling investments.
Virgo	Virgo advises us to focus on health-related matters, especially as it is the sign of food, nutrition, vitamins and herbs. It is also a time for organising or re-organising business affairs.

Libra	Libra is the sign of balance, fairness and harmony encouraging us to concentrate on partnerships, romance, justice, contracts, peace and diplomacy to bring about a better world.
Scorpio	This, the most mysterious sign of the zodiac and rules matters of death, rebirth, sex and transformation. The Scorpio Moon is an auspicious time under which to seek divine or psychic guidance.
Sagittarius	Sagittarius takes care of legal matters of all kinds, along with education and ethics. It is the sign that oversees long journeys and matters of faith, along with futuristic thinking and philosophy.
Capricorn	Capricorn is concerned with earthly matters such as career, business, reputation, results, honour, authority, achievement, recognition, governments and social standing. It also pricks our conscience and teaches us respect.
Aquarius	Aquarius is the humanitarian sign of the zodiac and brings into our awareness fairness, trustworthiness, objective judgement and reason. It also offers freedom, flashes of genius and general good luck.
Pisces	The Moon in Pisces takes care of the downtrodden in society. It is a time for increasing psychic ability, encouraging spiritual exploration and conquering fear.

Cool and serene She may appear in the night sky, but the extraordinary power of the Moon is felt throughout our world, and reaches into the very core of our being.

Mrs Darley Tale: The Gateway

'Are you all right dear?'

Mrs Darley's voice made me turn as I fumbled in my pocket for the elusive porch door key, which seemed to have become stuck in the lining of my coat.

I smiled. 'Yes, yes, I'm fine, thank you. Well, I will be when I can untangle my key.'

'Look, I've just boiled the kettle, why not come in from this persistent drizzle and join me for a cup of tea, then you can look for your key in the warmth of my cottage?'

'That would be lovely,' I said, picking up my briefcase from the step, and crossing the little patch of grass over to Mrs Darley's front steps.

As I entered her cottage, I was immediately greeted by the glowing fire, which made a welcome contrast from the damp, heavily misted autumn afternoon that threatened to close in as darkness settled.

I soon had the pocket of my waterproof turned inside out, and was still attempting to free the tangled key, when Mrs Darley came in from the kitchen carrying a tray which she set down on the small coffee table in front of the fire. I noticed at once that accompanying a rather large pot of Earl Grey tea was a plate of generously sized pieces of homemade shortbread.

'Any success with your key?'

I nodded. 'Yes…I think that's it.' I placed the freed key on top of my bag. 'Mmm, I must say, that shortbread looks delicious.'

'Well, don't thank me,' said Mrs Darley. 'Phyllis was up

early this morning baking for the Harvest Festival at the village hall, so these were her left over misshapen bits.'

'Well, long may her biscuits be misshapen,' I laughed, raising my welcome cup of tea in Phyllis' honour.

I closed my eyes as I took my first sip of tea, and sank back onto the little sofa with a sigh.

'That was a big sigh my dear, is everything all right?'

I opened my eyes.

'Yes, everything's fine.'

'You'll have to sound more convincing than that.'

'Everything is fine...really.'

'With the exception of?' she prompted gently.

It was useless trying to pretend with Mrs Darley of all people. 'With the exception of this promotion opportunity.'

She looked at me over the rim of her teacup.

'Are you still hesitating about stepping through the gateway?'

'The gateway?'

'The rune stones dear – you remember? You drew Thurisaz, the gateway?'

'Oh... yes... I'd forgotten... but now you mention it, no, I haven't stepped through that particular gateway as yet.'

'And what's stopping you from doing so?'

'Oh, a couple of things. The first being that I love the job I currently do, I meet nice people and I know what I'm doing...'

'So what you're saying is that your current job is comfortable?'

I nodded. 'Yes... I suppose it is.'

Mrs Darley regarded me thoughtfully. 'To be comfortable, my dear, is very nice, like wearing a pair of well-worn slippers, or getting into a warm bed, but sometimes we need more than nice. Sometimes we need to put on a pair of high heels that are decidedly uncomfortable but make us feel like a million dollars. Sometimes we need to get out of the warm bed and sleep beneath the night sky, so that we might stare in wonder at a star-covered canopy.'

I smiled at her colourful imagery.

'So what else is preventing you from stepping through the gateway?'

'Three of my colleagues also have their eye on the same promotion.'

'So?'

'So, it's awkward.'

'Why?'

'Well, two of them originally applied for the job I have at the moment, and although they're both very nice to me, I hear through the grapevine that it didn't go down too well when I was transferred in from another part of the country.'

'Indeed, but you must remember my dear that you all had an equal chance of getting that job, and likewise you will all have an equal chance of getting this new promotion.'

I sighed. 'Well yes, I expect so. In fact with this new position, we all have to take a psychometric test first, and only if we pass that will we get to the interview stage.'

'So, at the risk of repeating myself my dear – what's stopping you?'

She had a way of probing that often made me question my own reasoning. 'Well, when you put it like that... nothing I suppose.'

'If you don't mind me saying, you do sometimes seem to block your path with obstacles that are purely of your own making.'

I looked at her and smiled, knowing only too well that

she was right.

'And, don't forget, if you *are* successful in getting this promotion, your existing job will then become available for someone else.'

'I'd never thought of it like that,' I said. 'Perhaps I should step through that gateway then?'

'Ah, that's not for me to say, my dear. Only you can make such a decision, but we are in the waxing Moon phase – an auspicious time to take action, and as long as you have made your decision out of faith rather than fear, then all will be well.'

'What do you mean?'

'Well, we usually make decisions for one of two reasons, either from fear of trying something new, or from faith, that the new will be better than the old.'

'Then I will make my decision out of faith,' I said, surprised at how determined I sounded, 'and apply for the job tomorrow.'

'Just out of interest, when is the closing date?'

'Next Friday - at the end of the month.'

'Plenty of time then,' said Mrs Darley, getting up from her chair and reaching for a book that was tucked into the alcove shelves beside her.

'Well yes, I suppose so, but now I've made the decision, I may as well get on with it. I've got the application form in my briefcase, so after dinner tonight I might just sit down and ...'

I became aware however, that Mrs Darley wasn't really listening, but was busy flicking through a small blue book.

'Wednesday, dear,' she announced suddenly. 'That's the day to send in your application.'

'Why Wednesday?'

'Because the Moon, which will be waxing gibbous by then, will be in the sign of Capricorn.'

'And is that a good thing?' I asked.

'Why, of course. When the Moon passes through Capricorn, it is an auspicious time for job applications, career progression, and generally moving forward in the material world.'

'But how do you know where the Moon is going to be on Wednesday?'

'It's all in here, dear,' she said, retaking her seat and waving the small blue book in the air. 'In my zodiac diary.'

My interest was suddenly piqued. 'Oh. So how often does the Moon move into a new sign?'

'Approximately every two and a half days, meaning that it passes through every sign of the zodiac each lunar cycle.'

'That's fascinating. I mean, I know that the Sun moves through all the constellations each year, but I've never really thought about the Moon doing the same each month, and I had no idea that it could possibly affect us.'

'My dear, everything in the universe affects everything else, for everything is energy and everything is connected.'

'In that case I will certainly wait until next Wednesday before completing and submitting my application,' I promised.

Mrs Darley smiled. 'Then may the energies of a Capricorn Moon, carry your wishes to the gods my dear,' she said.

The following poem was written whilst contemplating the power that the Moon exerts, not only over our waters, but also over the earth itself. Moon and Earth are bound, like lovers who cannot bear to be separated, even though their relationship might eventually destroy them.

The Bond

I tremble in your presence,
As little by little
You tear me apart.
My veneer cracks,
My heart bleeds,
My soul lies broken,
And yet,
Powerless to break free,
We are bound for eternity.

Chapter Five

Moon Harvest

Mrs Darley Tale: The Gift Box

Awakened early by the Sun streaming onto my face, I left the comfort of my bed, made myself a cup of tea, and wandered out onto the front steps in order to drink in the splendour of a cool, but golden autumn morning.

'Hello dear.'

I quickly spun round to see Mrs Darley sitting on her doorstep, wrapped up warmly in a faded green shawl and holding a small trowel.

'Oh, good morning,' I laughed. 'I didn't see you there. You're gardening very early this morning, are you planting a window box?'

Mrs Darley shook her head, 'No, dear, more of a gift box.'

'That sounds nice. What's the occasion?'

'A funeral,' replied Mrs Darley. Her tone was surprisingly matter of fact as she went on pushing the dark purple bulbs into the soil.

'Oh.' I felt rather taken aback.

She lifted her head and smiled at me. 'Do I detect a note of surprise in your voice?'

'Er no…it's nice. Unusual but nice.' Privately, I felt that was an understatement. I'd never associated funerals or death with gift boxes before.

'I despair of all the wasted flowers at funerals,' said Mrs Darley, rising to her feet. 'It's all a big show on the day and then nothing, but the deceased always lives on in the hearts of those who loved them. This simple pot of bulbs, which will flower next spring, reflects that sentiment, especially one sown by the light of the waxing Moon.'

I looked skyward.

'Oh, you won't see Her now my dear. The sunlight is far too strong for us to be able to see the crescent Moon, but that doesn't mean that She isn't there. In fact, it's rather like those who have left this earthly plane, just because we can't see them doesn't mean to say they're not there.'

'Just hidden by a greater light?' I asked.

Mrs Darley smiled. 'Exactly.'

Reaping and Sowing

In the bible (Galatians 6:7), we are told by St Paul the Apostle,

'As ye sow, so shall ye reap.'

Now although we appreciate that this was not meant to be taken literally, these words have, nevertheless, been taken to heart by farmers and gardeners over millennia. Many believed, and still do, that if the Moon's cycles are strictly adhered to when sowing and harvesting crops and plants, then the growth, fruit, harvest, and overall quality of the produce will be far superior to those plants not having benefited from the same horticultural considerations.

Indeed, archaeologists have confirmed that lunar gardening has remained unchanged for thousands of years, as illustrated by some Sumerian texts. The ancients appreciated the correlation between the sowing, germinating, blooming, reaping and decay of plants, and the phases of the new, waxing, full, waning and dark Moon.

This important relationship between plant life and the Moon's cycles was also reflected by the way many Moon deities had responsibility for vegetation.

The North American Indians referred to the Moon as *'The old woman who never dies'*, and also knew her as *'Mother of the corn and vegetables.'* The Mexicans referred to Her as *'Great Mother of the Moon and waters'* and *'She of the maize plant'*. The Sumerian Moon God, Nanna or Sin, was called *'The Green One'*, *'The creator of the grasses'*, or *'Lord of the vegetables'*, and was often depicted as a tree with branches and a foliate face, very similar to our own European Green Man.

Nanna's daughter, Inanna, who eventually superseded Sin as the Sumerian Moon deity, was also a vegetation goddess, and often invoked as, *'Mistress of the field'*, or *'Mother of the vine stalk'*.

The origins of gardening by Moon lore is lost in the mists of time and has, until fairly recently, often been tucked away in the category of old wives' tales. In 1999 however, a TV series called *Supernatural*, began to change this misguided perception of lunar gardening, when it stated that the Moon really does have a profound influence on plants.

Subsequent research has shown that tree systems follow the lunar cycle by swelling and shrinking in much the same way as the oceanic tides. It is thought however, that in the case of trees, the Moon affects the electromagnetic field of the Earth, which in turn affects the fluid within the tree.

This is, of course, similar to the explanation given in Chapter 4, by Doctor Leonard Ravitz, who suggested that human behaviour does not change because of the Moon's pull of the fluid within our bodies, but rather that the gravitational pull of the Moon affects our own electromagnetic field or aura, which in turn affects our moods and well-being.

The following table provides an outline of gardening lore according to the Moon phases, and also gives a list of suggested horticultural activities to undertake as the Moon passes through its synodic cycle (when the sun and Moon come into alignment after twenty-nine and a half days), from new Moon to new Moon.

Moon Phase	Recommended Gardening Activities
New Moon to First Quarter	Sow seeds of all plants, except roots and tubers, to encourage upward growth. Sow and plant annuals to help them make short, shallow roots quickly. Sow grain of any kind. Plant crops that produce results outside of the plant. E.g. asparagus, broccoli, Brussel sprouts, cabbage, cauliflower, celery and cucumber. Graft plants, as the sap rises more quickly when the Moon is waxing. Mow, to encourage lush green growth.
First Quarter to Full	Sow seeds of all plants, except roots and tubers, to encourage upward growth. Sow grain. Plant vines, beans, pulses, peas, onions, peppers and tomatoes. Graft plants, as the sap rises more quickly when the Moon is waxing. Mow, to encourage lush green growth. Collect seeds, as they will be at their best coming up to the full Moon.
Full to Second Quarter	Plant biennials and perennials to help develop long, strong roots. Plant tubers, bulbs or root crops such as carrots, parsnips, radishes and turnips, to encourage downward growth.

	Plant trees and shrubs. Plant berried plants and potatoes. Begin rhubarb. Transplant, to enable the growing Moon to help plants grow strong. Harvest fruit and vegetables to enjoy them at their best.
Second Quarter to Dark	Plant tubers, bulbs or root crops such as carrots, parsnips, radishes and turnips to encourage downward growth. Weed, as new growth is subdued. Dig, plough, turn and cultivate the soil, to keep weeds at bay. Clear lawns, drains and guttering. Clear rubbish and drains, and ask for troublesome pests to leave. Mow, in order to slow growth. Make a garden fire and keep the ash to use as a mulch, or as a base for a compost heap. Harvest fruit and vegetables to enjoy them at their best.

The sowing of root crops under the waning Moon is well documented in 'Tusser's Husbandry' of 1580:

> *'Sowe peaseon and beanes in the wane of the Moone,*
> *Who soweth them sooner, he soweth too soone;*
> *That they with the planet, may rest and rise,*
> *And flourish, with bearing most plentiful wise.'*

In addition, trees, grain and yeast are also affected by the Moon, and Plutarch tells us:

The Moone showeth her power most evidently even in those bodies, which have neither sense nor lively breath; for carpenters reject the timber of trees fallen in the ful-moone, as being soft and tender, subject also to the worme and putrefaction, and that quickly, by reason of excessive moisture; husbandmen, likewise.

Make haste to gather up their wheat and other grain from the threshing-floore, in the wane of the moone, and toward the end of the month, that beinge hardened thus with the drinesse, the heape in the garner may keepe the better from beinge fustie, and continue the longer; whereas corne which is inned and laied up at the full moone, by reason of the softnesse and over-much moisture, of all other, doth most crackle and burst.

It is commonly said also, that if a leaven (yeast) be laied in the ful-moone, the paste will rise and take leaven better.

The waning Moon was often considered an inauspicious time for picking certain produce. In Devon it was thought that apples would 'shrump up' or wither, whilst in Essex the following rhyme was adhered to with regards to picking mushrooms.

'When the moon is at the full,
Mushrooms you may freely pull
But when the moon is on the wane,
Wait 'ere you think to pluck again.

In sharp contrast, the French believed that the only time oak trees could be successfully felled, was during the waning Moon when the wind was in the north.

According to the late nineteenth century German mystic and philosopher, Rudolph Steiner (the forerunner of what is now known as 'Biodynamic gardening'), horticulturalists should not only take into account the phase of the Moon when planning their garden activities, but also its astronomical position.

   We have seen that the Moon travels through all twelve signs of the zodiac during its twenty-nine-and-a-half-day orbit around the Earth, spending approximately two and a half days in each. Every sign however, is also governed by one of the four elements of Air, Fire, Water and Earth, each of which also has a bearing on certain aspects of plant growth. Steiner said these considerations were vital if a plant was to fulfil its potential.

Astrological Sign of the Moon	Element	Affects Development of:
Taurus, Virgo, Capricorn	Earth	Root
Gemini, Libra, Aquarius	Air	Flower
Cancer, Scorpio, Pisces	Water	Leaf
Leo, Aries, Sagittarius	Fire	Fruit and seed

The table below provides more detailed information with regards to the specific zodiacal sign that the Moon happens to be transiting.

Astrological Sign of the Moon and the Relevant Element	Recommended Gardening Activity
Aries (Fire)	An Aries Moon calls us to harvest and store all fruits and root crops such as potatoes, swedes, turnips carrots, parsnips and beetroot. Use the power of this fire sign to light fires and burn garden rubbish.

Taurus (Earth)	This is the second-best zodiacal sign in which to plant and transplant. Root crops and leafy vegetables seem to respond particularly well to a Taurean Moon. It is recommended that hardy flowers are planted during this Moon phase as they should flourish.
Gemini (Air)	This is another auspicious time to harvest root vegetables and fruit. Destroy weeds and ask pests to leave. Gemini is a dry barren air sign and does not favour planting or sowing.
Cancer (Water)	When the Moon is in the sign of Cancer, the time is right for grafting, irrigation, transplanting and planting, especially asparagus, sprouts, sage, cabbage, beetroot, cauliflower, spinach, parsley and carrots. Flowers planted now will do well. Do not cut wood as it will be too wet.
Leo (Fire)	Leo is the most barren sign in the zodiac, therefore weeding and burning garden rubbish is recommended. Other tidying duties and maintenance of gardening equipment can also be undertaken. If lawn growth needs to be restrained, now is the time to mow. The harvesting of root crops and fruit for storage is recommended.

Virgo (Earth)	Although Virgo is an Earth sign, it is one that is barren and moist and not recommended for planting. Some spring flowers however, such as crocuses, daffodils and snowdrops should do well as will vines.
Libra (Air)	Libra is one of the best signs in which to plant beautiful fragrant flowers, grape vines, clematis and herbs. It is also a good time to plant root crops of any variety.
Scorpio (Water)	Scorpio is the best sign under which to plant sturdy plants and vines. Tomatoes respond well to being transplanted under this sign as do corn, bulbs and squash. It is a very beneficial sign for transplanting, irrigation and grafting, especially during a Scorpio waning Moon.
Sagittarius (Fire)	Sagittarius is another dry barren sign, so the time should be used to cultivate the soil, although leeks, onions and shallots usually do well when planted under this sign.
Capricorn (Earth)	A Capricorn Moon is good for planting root crops and tomatoes as both do well at this time. This is an excellent time for grafting and cutting back as the plant appears to heal quite quickly. Apply organic fertilizer during this phase.

Aquarius (Air)	Aquarius is a very barren and dry sign and as such it is a time for cleaning drains and guttering, although both root and fruit crops can be harvested. Soil cultivation is recommended, but planting should be avoided until the Moon enters the more beneficial sign of Pisces.
Pisces (Water)	The sign of Pisces encourages all root growth. Almost anything can be planted under this sign and thrive, although it is especially indicated for celery and rhubarb. Most flowers and seeds planted under this Moon sign will grow well. It is also a good time for irrigation.

Naturally, the seasons, the weather, and the type of soil, must all be taken into account in order for any horticultural venture to be successful.

An old adage that may prove useful for those who are worried about being caught out by the first frost of the season, is as follows:

'Frost at the dark moon will kill fruit and blossoms, but frosts in the light of the moon will not.'

The great seventeenth century herbalist, physician and astrologer, Nicholas Culpeper, provided us with a wealth of knowledge on the description, environment, season, applications, and governing planet, of a wide variety of herbs and plants. From his writings, we can ascertain which plants are ruled specifically by the Moon, for use in both healing and ritual.

Please note:
The suggestions and uses that follow were made by Culpeper in the mid 1600's. Please consult your G.P. in the first instance if you are in ill health. Should you wish to take herbal remedies please ensure that you consult a qualified herbalist.

Agrimony

This lovely lemon flowered plant is a gout, liver and bowel cleanser, which also heals cuts and bruises, soothes coughs and draws out boils and splinters.

In Guernsey, young girls would sleep with two, nine-leafed fronds of the plant under their pillow, secured with a new pin, in order to dream of their future husband.

Clary Sage

This precious herb was once used to cleanse the eyes, soothe skin disorders, and to ease the pain of sciatica, gout and arthritis.

It was often known as 'Clear eye' or 'Christ's eye', for when the seeds were soaked in water, they formed a thick gel, which helped draw out grit and debris from the eye.

N.B. Do not use Clary Sage Essential Oil in, or near the eyes

Cress (Water)

This salad favourite was once used to prevent scurvy, due to its high vitamin C content. It was thought to encourage the flow of urine, and helped to eliminate freckles, spots and pimples. It was also hailed as a blood cleanser, and used to clear a 'muddled mind'.

Due to its peppery taste, it was considered invaluable in

reviving cooled passions stemming from familiarity with a long-term partner.

Cucumber

A popular salad ingredient, cucumber was invaluable in the treatment of inflamed conditions of the liver, stomach and eyes. It was used to remove redness from the face, and to promote the flow of urine.

It was thought that by planting cucumbers at the Summer Solstice, larger vegetables would result, albeit cucumbers planted by elderly people would not grow so well.

Iris

This beautiful flower was a valuable astringent, which was used to regulate bleeding of all kinds, and clear external ulcers.

Orris Root comes from the iris, and because of its delicate violet perfume, was said to repel musty odours from stored linen. It was also chewed by those fond of tobacco and garlic to drive away the smell.

The fifth century French King, Clovis, was aware of the fact that the iris only grew in shallow water and upon spotting a clump of them growing alongside a body of water, was able to lead his Merovingian army safely away from the Goths. He then took the iris as his symbol and this later became the French Fleur de Lys.

Lady's Smock (Cuckoo Flower)

As a relation of watercress, lady's smock has similar properties. It was used to help prevent scurvy, assist in the flow of urine, and to eliminate freckles, spots and pimples. It was also thought to cleanse the blood, and clear a muddled head.

This lilac-coloured flower is a plant of the fairies and is best left well alone according to legend. If a May garland was found to contain lady's smock by mistake, the whole garland would have to be redone as it was considered bad luck to annoy the elementals.

Lettuce

Lettuce was generally thought to cool inflamed conditions, combat insomnia, and ease both headaches and constipation. It was also said to quench the thirst, and increase milk in breast-feeding women.

For all its medicinal properties however, lettuce has a very poor reputation in the realms of love and fertility. It was said that when Adonis died, Venus threw herself on a lettuce leaf to cool her ardour.

Growing too much lettuce was thought to prevent conception, and Elizabethan women who tired of childbirth, ate copious amounts of lettuce to bring about the end of their reproductive days. It was once thought that even standing on a lettuce leaf would cause a miscarriage.

Lily

Lilies were used to settle the mind and encourage rest, whilst also having the ability to heal skin disorders and combat cystitis.

Anyone carrying a lily was considered safe from snake bites, and legend tells us that the first lily is said to have sprung from Eve's tears as she left the Garden of Eden after being tempted by the serpent.

The lily was a noted cure for corns, and the Romans planted them close to their army camps in order to prevent their soldiers' feet from becoming sore.

Moonwort

This rare herb was once recommended for healing wounds of all kinds. It was also used to arrest bleeding, mend ruptures and dispel vomiting.

Legend has it that it has the power to open locks and unshoe any horse that treads upon it.

Mouse-ear Hawkweed

This white flowered and downy haired plant, was once used to counteract jaundice, kidney stones and bowel disorders. It was also used to stem bleeding, soothe coughs, and heal ulcers, sores and ruptures.

Mouse-ear hawkweed was also called the 'herb of nails', and many blacksmiths tucked a sprig of the herb into a horse's bridle when it was being shoed, to keep the horse still and prevent any injuries occurring in the smithy.

Orpine

Orpine was seldom used internally, but had a marked effect when used externally upon inflammation, burns and wounds.

Young girls would push a sprig of orpine into the crack of their doors on mid summer's eve, and according to whether it fell to the left or right, would determine her lover's intention.

> *'Oft on the shrub she casts her eye,*
> *That spoke her true love's secret sign,*
> *Or else, alas! Too plainly told,*
> *Her true love's faithless heart was cold.'*

Some would hang a piece of orpine in their home and as long as it remained green, good health would be theirs.

Poppy

Poppies have always been known for their ability to encourage sleep and ease respiratory problems. They were once used to soothe stomach upsets, cool inflammation, and ease toothache.

If picked, poppies were said to induce headaches and blindness, in addition to attracting thunder-bolts. They are associated with remembrance, having sprung up in the fields of Flanders one hundred years after the Battle of Waterloo.

Rose (White)

Rose has always been known for its cooling and drying properties, with the white rose being far more effective than the coloured varieties. Being a powerful astringent, rose was used to bind and heal wounds, although it was not recommended for internal use.

White roses have long been associated with the Virgin Mary and are still carried at her religious festivals. The Yorkists took the white rose as their emblem in the War of the Roses in 1455, whilst the Lancastrians favoured the red rose. If the white rose blooms in late summer, it was said to be a bad omen, and in Dorset it was considered bad luck to even smell one.

Wallflower

According to Galen, a second century Greek physician, surgeon and philosopher, yellow wallflowers were considered more powerful than other colour. They were said to cleanse the blood and liver, act as a tonic to the reproductive system, strengthen the joints and ease all aches and pains, including gout.

In the West Country, red wallflowers were referred to as 'bloody warriors' due to their rich colour.

Willow

The graceful willow was used as an analgesic, and prevented wounds from excessive bleeding. It helped to ease colic, calm the libido, encourage the production of urine, and rid the hair of dandruff.

It was however, considered unlucky to cut willow, except for palm crosses on Easter Sunday which, when blessed, were said to protect against disease, thunder and lightning.

Today, there is a wealth of knowledge available about lunar gardening, and many studies have been carried out to illustrate the beneficial effects of performing specific horticultural tasks during different phases and zodiacal placements of the Moon.

To our ancestors however, scientific studies were neither available nor necessary, for they simply understood and accepted, due to centuries of use, which activities to carry out beneath a particular Moon phase. In the words of Plutarch:

'The moone showeth her power most evidently even in those bodies, which have neither sense nor lively breath.'

Mrs Darley Tale: The Pilgrimage

Calling round to Mrs Darley's cottage on my way back from work one afternoon in late October, I found Lucy curled up on the chair beside the fire with a glass of blackberry juice and a notepad.

'Come in and join us, dear,' said Mrs Darley, 'Lucy and I have just finished discussing a school project she has to do.'

'Oh no, I won't stay,' I said, 'I don't want to disturb you. I only came to ask if you would let the plumber in for me tomorrow. I've got a leak under the sink.'

'Of course dear, of course, that's no problem.'

'Thank you, I really appreciate it.' I turned to Lucy who was just draining the last of her juice. 'So what's your project about?'

'We have to write about a local person, dead or alive, who did something interesting, then we're putting on a show at the end of term, to tell parents and friends what we found out, and to remember people we might otherwise have forgotten about.' said Lucy.

'What a lovely idea. So who have you chosen?'

'Daniel Gumb.'

The name was totally unfamiliar. 'And who is he?' I asked.

'*Was*, dear,' corrected Mrs Darley. 'He was born at the beginning of the eighteenth century.'

'Oh.' I said, feeling rather foolish.

'He was a man who lived in the middle of the moor, and we're going up to see his house on Friday afternoon after school before it gets too dark,' said Lucy, getting up from the chair and pulling on her coat. 'You can come,' she added, kindly.

'That would be lovely,' I said, 'and thank you for asking

me, but I don't think I'll be back from work in time.'

'That's settled then, we'll all meet here just before five o clock on Friday,' said Mrs Darley, as she ushered us both towards the door, almost as though she hadn't heard a word I'd said.

***

My early afternoon appointment on Friday went surprisingly smoothly and I found myself able to leave in plenty of time to meet Mrs Darley, Lucy, Rose and Bod for our five o'clock sojourn onto the moor.

To my surprise, we didn't walk onto the moor from the direction of our cottages, but all climbed into Bod's old white van, and set off for the village of Minions at the top of the lane.

'It's a much easier walk from here,' said Bod, as we pulled into the little car park and grabbed our coats, scarves and gloves, along with a couple of rucksacks. 'At least we can follow the old railway track most of the way, which means that it's more or less a flat walk, and it'll be better for the return journey in the dark.'

I hadn't really considered the return journey, and suddenly wondered how I would feel about wandering around on the moor after sundown. I did my best however, to put these unsettling thoughts to the back of my mind and concentrate on walking over the old granite blocks that once carried the railway sleepers.

After following the track for half a mile or so, we veered away to the left, and began picking our way over the granite boulders that littered the moor. This was a poignant reminder of the harsh days of tin and copper mining, when lives were both cruel and short, and I suddenly felt as though I was on a pilgrimage to honour those who had walked the land before me. In an instant however, my attention was diverted, as Lucy gave a shout.

'I can see it.'

As we joined her at the top of the ridge, we could just make out the mouth of what looked like a gaping doorway in the near distance.

'Come on.' Lucy began to run across the open moorland and within a few minutes, we were all standing outside the strange granite shelter that was known as Daniel Gumb's Cave.

'Goodness me,' I said, peering inside, 'did he really live in here with his wife and family?'

'Oh no, dear,' said Mrs Darley, 'this is a reconstruction. His original home would have been somewhere over there.' She waved her hand vaguely towards the now abandoned Cheesewring quarry.

'What happened to his original home?'

'Sadly, it was destroyed when the quarry was extended in 1873. Luckily though, all was not lost, for some sympathetic quarrymen managed to save one of the roof stones with the original Pythagorean diagram carved into it by Mr Gumb himself.'

'A Pythagorean diagram? What's that?' Asked Rose.

Mrs Darley smiled. 'Your daughter will tell you.'

'*Everyone* knows Pythagoras' theorem,' said Lucy, pleased to be given an opportunity to show off her knowledge. 'We did it in school. It's about right-angled triangles.'

Rose shrugged. 'I'm none the wiser.'

'The square of the length of the hypotenuse is equal to the sum of the square of the other two sides,' said Bod, laughing at the surprised look on Lucy's face.

'You know about it?' She asked, clearly amazed that her father would know such a thing.

'Some things you just never forget.'

'Well, I must have missed that lesson,' laughed Rose.

'Never mind, dear,' said Mrs Darley. She turned to me. 'Why don't you and Lucy climb up onto the roof stone and take a look before the Sun sets and the light is gone?'

As the Sun began to disappear over the western moor, Lucy and I climbed up onto the granite roof, where she made a sketch of the diagram that Daniel Gumb had carved so laboriously over two centuries ago. Meanwhile, I sat and pondered on why he had felt the need to carve such a diagram on the roof of his unusual home.

With Lucy's diagram complete, we climbed down from the roof and returned to the group below, where Bod had lit a small camping stove, over which sat a boiling kettle.

'This is a nice surprise,' I said, as we huddled around the stove in what was now a cool wind, and the advancing darkness of an early October evening.

'Well, here's another one, courtesy of Rose,' said Mrs Darley, as she offered round a plate of Rose's delicious pasties and poured a tot of whiskey from her hip flask into all the adults' mugs of tea. 'Let us raise our mugs and drink to this unusual place, and I will tell you the strange tale of Daniel Gumb.'

We all settled ourselves amid the crumbs of the pasties, whilst holding onto the remnants of our mugs of tea for warmth, and waited for Mrs Darley to begin.

'Daniel Gumb,' she said, 'was born in the early eighteenth century, not far from here in the parish of Linkinhorne and was said to be a good scholar with a gentle disposition. In his adult life, he worked as a moorland stonecutter, and eventually decided to build himself a house here on the moor, in the place he loved, and out of the granite he loved.'

'How wonderful if we could just build ourselves something, anywhere we liked,' said Rose longingly.

'The country would end up looking a bit of a mess though, love,' said Bod.

'Yes, I suppose it would,' replied Rose. 'Sorry, Mrs D, do go on.'

The roof of Daniel Gumb's cave on Bodmin Moor, showing his carved illustration of Pythagoras' Theorem

'Well, it is thought that Daniel married three times. His first wife was someone called Joan, about whom very little is known. His second wife was called Thomasine, and is believed to have died in childbirth, whilst his third wife, Florence, came to live with him in his moorland home, and bore him many children.'

'Good grief,' said Rose, 'and they all lived here? In a house this size?'

'Well, as I said, the original house was destroyed so we can't be too sure of its exact size,' said Mrs Darley, 'but we must remember, Rose dear, that life was so much simpler in those days. Children played outside and they didn't need as much room as we do in order to accommodate our ever-growing collection of material things. They were also accustomed to living together in close proximity.'

Rose nodded. 'I suppose so. No wardrobes full of clothes, no labour-saving kitchen appliances, and certainly no fancy bathrooms.'

'I'm glad I didn't live then,' said Lucy with feeling.

'Anyway,' Mrs Darley continued, 'although Daniel Gumb may have been perceived by some to just be a simple stonecutter, he was in fact, a very intelligent man. He loved mathematics and used his roof stones as an observatory, from where he studied the heavens.'

'Hence the carvings up there on the roof I suppose?' Asked Bod, peering at his daughter's drawing in the diminishing light.'

'Indeed,' said Mrs Darley. 'Daniel gained the nickname of *The Mountain Philosopher*', and although he had the reputation of being rather eccentric, he was often sought after for his vast knowledge. In fact, in the mid 1700's he was asked to draw up plans for the local surveyor's office, and his plan of Twelve Men's Moor, which lies just over there,' said Mrs Darley waving her hand towards the west, 'can still be seen in the County Record Office.'

'That's amazing,' I said, wondering why I had never heard of this man before.

'It is, my dear, yes, but there's also a more mysterious side to Daniel Gumb.'

Lucy's eyes widened. 'Ooo, what?'

'Well, Daniel Gumb kept a daily diary, which was found many years after his death, by the famous Vicar of Morwenstowe, the Reverend Robert Hawker. And, according to this diary, Daniel Gumb received a very strange visitor one hot summer's day in 1764.'

Lucy's whole body tensed with excitement. 'Who?'

'Well Lucy, one day when Daniel was attending to his stonecutting duties, he suddenly became aware of a stranger standing beside him, and as he looked up to greet the man, he noticed something most odd.'

'What?' asked Lucy, anxious to move the story along.

'The stranger appeared to be dressed in outdated clothes that would have been fashionable long before Daniel Gumb's own time.

'The stranger spoke to Daniel, addressing him by name, and sympathised with the hard work he had to endure. Daniel, although puzzled as to how the stranger knew his name, agreed that the work was hard, but said it was necessary in order to feed his family. Then, the stranger said something that made Daniel Gumb's blood run cold.'

'What?' Asked Lucy eagerly. 'What did he say?'

Mrs Darley leaned forward and whispered into the growing darkness.

'"Daniel", he said, "man carries out his labours until the evening comes. When will it be nightfall for Daniel Gumb?"'

I shivered, and clasped my hands around what remained of my mug of tea for warmth as Mrs Darley continued with her tale.

'Feeling rather disturbed by the stranger, Daniel bent his head for a second to collect his thoughts as to how to reply, but when he looked up, the stranger was gone, just as if he had vanished into thin air.'

'Was he a ghost?' Whispered Lucy.

'Perhaps.'

The darkness seemed to close in around us, becoming almost tangible, and my imagination danced out into the black abyss, conjuring up sinister strangers from centuries past.

'Look!' shouted Bod.

The mug that I had held onto so tightly for warmth, instantly slipped from my hands and shattered noisily on the granite boulder below, as the fear of ghostly apparitions rattled my nerves.

'I'm so sorry,' I said, making a pathetic attempt to pick

up the broken pieces and stow them away in an empty paper bag.

'Oh don't worry about the mug,' said Bod, as he stood up on one of the granite boulders and pointed into the blackness. 'Just look over there – that's far more interesting.'

We all looked past his outstretched arm and watched as the waxing gibbous Moon began to rise in the east over the high peaks of Dartmoor.

'Ah,' sighed Mrs Darley, scrambling to her feet, 'I wonder how many times Daniel Gumb's eyes would have looked upon that same Moonrise?'

This unanswerable question hung in the chill evening air, until Mrs Darley finally broke the silence.

'Come, everyone,' she said, as she began packing away the remains of our feast, 'it is time to go. The Blood Moon has risen to see Her children safely home.'

Acts of ritual celebration or magick, lend themselves to being performed beneath the Moon's full light, whilst clandestine meetings and covert activities lend themselves to the cover provided by the dark Moon. What we often forget however, is that the Moon is always there, regardless of whether we can see Her or not. She is always the silent witness.

Silent Witness

I am the silent witness,
She who sees all.

The lover's tryst,
The wreckers' lights,
The smugglers' haul,
And sacred rites.

I am both friend and foe.
I am the silent witness.

Chapter Six

Moon Magick

Mrs Darley Tale: The Moon Line

It was eight o clock, and daylight was yielding to dusk on an early October evening, as I pulled into my allotted parking space at the edge of the moor. I got out of the car and lifted my briefcase out of the boot in order to tackle a mound of paperwork before allowing myself the luxury of supper and bed.

As I locked the car, I was suddenly aware of voices, and the unmistakable sound of Mrs Darley's laughter drifting across the lane.

'Hello,' I called, as she opened the five-barred gate and began to walk up the slope towards me.

'Oh, hello dear, I didn't see you there. Have you had a good day?'

'Yes,' I said. 'It's been good, but busy.'

'So, don't you think you've done enough for today? She asked, pointing to the briefcase in my hand.

'I suppose so, but I really need to finish a few things off before I go in to work tomorrow.'

'And what will happen if you don't?'

I shrugged. I had sometimes wondered of course, if my work-life balance had become rather one-sided, but I tried not to think about it too much. My neighbour however, was waiting for an answer, and I knew she wasn't going to let me off the hook. 'Well, nothing I suppose, but the paperwork will just keep piling up.'

'You know, it seems to me that at the very least you need a break - isn't that right, Peter?' she turned and smiled at her rather good-looking, silver haired companion who was walking across the lane to join us.

'Absolutely right,' said Peter, 'you do need a break. Why don't you come with us?'

'Come with you? Why, where are you going?' I asked, my curiosity piqued.

'Dozmary Pool,' said Mrs Darley.

'What, over the other side of the moor?' I asked, unable to keep the note of surprise out of my voice.

Peter laughed. 'It's not *that* far. Come on, leave your briefcase in your car and jump into my Land Rover.'

'But I'm not dressed for the moor, I'm still in my suit and I…'

My protests however, were waved aside. 'We won't be walking too far in the dark,' said Mrs Darley, 'and we'll only be out for an hour or so.'

Feeling somewhat outnumbered and not quite knowing how to refuse, I put my briefcase back into the boot of my car and climbed into the back seat of Peter's Land Rover.

Very soon, we were following the narrow road that traced the River Fowey towards Bolventor. Darkness had now fallen, and as we headed out towards Dozmary Pool, the waxing gibbous Moon rose high in the sky, highlighting the barrenness of the wild open moor and almost transforming it into a magickal kingdom.

After a mile or so, Peter pulled into a roughly hewn parking area on the right-hand side of the road. He switched off the engine and I took this as my cue to get out, where I stood shivering in the cool night air. Mrs Darley soon joined me, took my arm and led me towards the dry-stone wall.

'There,' she said, pointing across the top of the wall,

'Dozmary Pool.'

'It's beautiful,' I whispered, as my eyes fell upon the silvered waters of the moonlit lake. It was so still, I could almost have convinced myself it was a mirror, fashioned by the Greek Demi-God, Narcissus, so that he might forever admire his beauty.

'And magickal,' she added, 'for this is the place where legends are made, the most famous of which concerns that of King Arthur's sword Excalibur.'

'Is this where it's supposed to lie?' I asked, feeling a sudden surge of excitement.

'According to Cornish legend certainly, although many will lay claim to it being in Wales or Glastonbury.'

'But how did it get here?'

'It was said that after the battle of Camlann, just as Sir Bedivere was carrying the injured King Arthur away, Arthur made Bedivere promise to cast his beautiful sword, Excalibur, into this lake. Initially, Bedivere agreed to Arthur's request, but when the moment came to throw the sword into the lake, he couldn't bring himself to do it, and decided he would hide it instead. Upon returning to Arthur, the dying king immediately asked Bedivere what he had seen as he cast the sword into the water, to which Bedivere replied, 'Nothing'.

'I think I might have been tempted to do the same,' I said. 'I wouldn't have wanted to give up Excalibur, either.'

'Ah, but you can't fool the king,' said Mrs Darley, 'especially a king such as Arthur, and Bedivere's answer was enough for Arthur to know that his wishes had not been carried out.'

'So what did he do?'

'He immediately sent Bedivere back to the lake to carry out his instructions. Once again however, just as Bedivere stood on the edge of the lake, he simply couldn't bring himself to throw the sword into the water, and once again he hid it before returning to the king.'

'Not a good idea to attempt it twice,' I said.

'Indeed not, and of course, just as before, Arthur asked Bedivere what he had seen upon casting the sword into the water. The poor knight finally realised that he had little choice other than to return to the pool to carry out his king's wishes.'

'At last,' I sighed, totally caught up in this wonderful tale.

'Standing here, at the side of the lake, Bedivere reluctantly threw the magnificent Excalibur into the waters, and watched as it disappeared below the surface.'

For a moment none of us spoke, and the Moon shone on the waters, just as it had since King Arthur's time.

'And then?' I prompted, certain this couldn't be the end of the story.

'And then, just as Bedivere was about to turn away, he saw an arm slowly rise from the water, brandishing the sword three times in the air, before sinking back into the dark watery depths.'

'The Lady of the Lake, I presume?'

'In some versions of the story yes, whilst in others she is described as more of an enchantress and a sorcerer,' said Mrs Darley as she stared out wistfully across the water, before bringing her attention back to the moment.

'Anyway, my dear, it is believed that this is where the sword will stay, until Arthur rises again. Oh, look,' she added, suddenly pointing across the pool, 'there's the Moon Line.'

'The Moon Line?' I echoed, half expecting to see a ghostly arm waving in the moonlight from the depths of the water. 'What's that exactly?'

'It's when the silver line of the Moon's light reflects upon the surface of the water - like that.' Mrs Darley pointed towards the centre of the lake.

I turned my head to follow her outstretched hand, and saw a rippled line of moonlight reflecting in the water, almost as though it was attempting to divide the lake in two. 'It's beautiful,' I said.

'Well, my dear,' said Mrs Darley, 'whenever you see the Moon Line, you should make a wish.'

'And that,' said Peter, 'is exactly what we have come here tonight to do.'

I saw Mrs Darley look across at Peter and smile, and for a moment, I felt as though I was intruding.

'Come, my dear,' she said, as though suddenly remembering me, 'let us all take a moment and think about the wish we would like to make.'

And so we stood, in the cool autumn air, looking out over the silvered waters, each of us lost in our own thoughts, whilst for the briefest of moments, I fancied that I could almost see the hand that held Excalibur rising from the lake. It was so enchanting and romantic that I yearned to have someone to share it with.

'Now,' said Mrs Darley, breaking the silence and pressing a five pence piece into my hand, 'take this silver coin and make your wish as you cast it into the water. But remember – your wish must come from the heart.'

I nodded and turned back to face the water, casting my wish, along with the silver coin into the enchanted lake.

Moon Magick

The Moon has been synonymous with magick since time began, not least because moonlight changes our consciousness, one of the most important things we aim to achieve when crafting magick. The Moon softens our outer persona, yet strengthens what lies within. She inspires us to dance and drum, sing and chant, yet encourages quiet reflection. She invites us to play with the wind and call to the gods, yet bids us listen to the wisdom of the universe.

The Moon is magick, and magick is enchanting. It takes us far beyond the trials of everyday life and sets us in a place where anything is possible, where dreams can become reality, and where we are encouraged to believe in ourselves.

Although my real introduction to magick came much later in mine and Mrs Darley's relationship, I feel it is important at this point to explore the importance of the Moon's phases in a magickal context. This will enable us to appreciate how we might harness her powerful energies to enhance our magick, and to open up our minds to the liberating process of self-change and mastery.

Since man first walked the Earth, he has used the phases of the Moon, and invoked lunar deities – both male and female – to bring his magickal desires to fruition.

Nowadays, the majority of those who reside in the west, acknowledge the Moon as a feminine energy, often portrayed as a cup or chalice that constantly fills and empties. She is gentle in nature, but strong in effect, despite yielding in visibility to the stronger light of the Sun, Her masculine consort. The Sun however, is relatively simple in nature compared to the complexities of our ever-changing Moon.

The Moon, as already discussed, is in a constant state of flux as it waxes and wanes each month, and as such, offers us the opportunity to practice our magick for a wide variety of purposes, dependent upon its phase.

It is not however, only the Moon phase that is important when practicing lunar magick, but also the constellation in which the Moon happens to be at any given time. We saw in Chapter 4 that the Moon moves into a new constellation approximately every two and a half days, a fact which can impact considerably on the type of magick that is practised. The table below provides a basic indication of beneficial zodiacal influences with regards to magickal intent.

Astrological Sign Housing the Moon	Beneficial for Magick Involving:
Aries	Leadership, authority, rebirth, willpower, general health, vitality and resolving conflict situations. Healing of the head, brain and face.
Taurus	Love, romance, property, money, material assets, security, self-esteem, fertility, strength, patience, success in music, the arts and business. Healing of the neck, throat and ears.
Gemini	Communication, moving home, writing, travel, memory improvement, commerce, children, teaching and learning. Healing of the shoulders, arms, hands and lungs.
Cancer	Home, family, psychic gifts and gardening. Healing of the chest and abdomen.
Leo	Power, authority, courage, fertility, childbirth, love, romance, creativity, self-expression, investments and holidays. Healing of cervical spine and heart.

Virgo	Employment, intellect, health, diet, medicine, business and matters of law. Healing of intestines, thoracic spine and nervous system.
Libra	Artistic pursuits, justice, partnerships, emotional balance, peace, love, marriage, diplomacy. Healing of lumbar spine and kidneys.
Scorpio	Sex, psychic matters, secrets, transformation, morals and truth. Healing of the reproductive organs.
Sagittarius	Publications, legal matters, travel, truth, learning, philosophy, ethics, dreams, spirituality and new beginnings. Healing of liver, thighs and hips.
Capricorn	Organisation, ambition, recognition, career, politics, business, achievement, awards, leadership and social standing. Healing of knees, bones, teeth and skin.
Aquarius	Science, freedom, creativity, problem solving, friendship, teamwork, breaking habits and addictions and hope. Healing of the calves, ankles and blood.

Pisces	Clairvoyance, intuition, music, creative arts, the underdogs of society, retrieving lost items, journeying within, charities and psychic healing. Healing of the feet and lymph glands.

The popular depiction of the Moon's phases as Maiden, Mother and Crone has captured the imagination of many modern-day Pagans, and is undoubtedly an excellent comparison of the lunar cycle to the three ages of women. The phases can also be applied to men, in the roles of Son, Protector and Elder.

This is however, a relatively modern concept, having been created by J. G. Frazer, in his 1890 book, *The Golden Bough,* and later expanded upon by the late Margaret Murray, a British Egyptologist and anthropologist. It is undoubtedly a profoundly stirring analogy that will live on in the psyche of many who feel an affinity with the Moon.

On a personal level, I have always felt that there is something missing from these three ages of men and women. To move from Maiden to Mother and from Mother to Crone, or from Son to Protector and Protector to Elder are huge steps. This is like the Moon moving from new crescent to full, and full to dark, without the waxing and waning phases in between. I have therefore added the phase of Enchantress between Maiden and Mother to align with the waxing Moon, and added the phase of Wise Woman between Mother and Crone, to align with the waning Moon. These are set out in the table below, along with what I feel are suitable male equivalents.

Moon Phase	Female Life Phase	Male Life Phase
New Moon	Maiden	Son
Waxing Moon	Enchantress	Warrior
Full Moon	Mother	Protector
Waning Moon	Wise Woman	Sage
Dark Moon	Crone	Elder

The phases of the Moon and the constellations through which She travels, constantly offer new opportunities to plan, grow, achieve, and reflect on all aspects of our lives, presenting us with a sky of unrivalled beauty under which we are able to perform our magick.

Mrs Darley Tale: Selene

I shivered and pulled my cardigan tightly around my shoulders as I stood waiting for Mrs Darley to open the door one chilly autumn evening.

'Hello dear,' said Mrs Darley, throwing the door open wide, 'you look frozen. Come in, come in, you know you don't have to stand on ceremony here.'

Gratefully I stepped inside, and allowed the welcoming warmth of her lovely cottage to envelop me. The doors of the wood burner were open and the logs crackled and hissed with the heat. On the left-hand side of the hearth stood a beautiful vase of deep orange chrysanthemums in recognition of the autumn season, whilst to the right, a group of three golden pillar candles burned brightly.

'Ah,' said Mrs Darley, who was still standing at the open door, 'I see you've brought Selene with you.'

I turned, puzzled, half expecting to see someone else enter the cottage. 'Who's Selene?'

'Why the Moon, dear. Selene is the Greek Moon

Goddess.'

A wave of embarrassment suddenly washed over me for not remembering who She was. The previous year, at the festival of Samhain, I had attended a rather moving ceremony in Mrs Darley's garden, where we had scattered the ashes of her brother-in-law Tommy, to the four winds. With the scattering complete, Mrs Darley had asked that Tommy's soul rise on the wings of the Moon Goddess, Selene.

'Yes, of course,' I said, 'I do remember now, but I'm afraid I don't really know anything about Her.'

'Well, my dear, sit down, have a glass of wine and we will talk of Selene some more.'

I immediately made myself comfortable in my favourite fireside chair, and accepted a glass of deep rich claret from Mrs Darley's outstretched hand.

'Selene,' began Mrs Darley, as she settled back in her chair, 'was the daughter of the Titan god, Hyperion, and his sister, Theia. She was a beautiful child and as She grew up, her beauty attracted the attention of the all-powerful Greek God, Zeus, whom you and I have talked of before. Mind you, dear,' she said, leaning forward as though we were conspirators, 'that's nothing new – Zeus was attracted to most beautiful women. Anyway, the union of Zeus and Selene resulted in three children, much to the displeasure of his wife Hera.'

I laughed. 'I'm not surprised. I would probably have been a little miffed myself.'

'Well,' said Mrs Darley, 'Hera was what one might call a long-suffering wife, but I don't suppose it would have been any comfort to her to know that Selene never really loved Zeus.'

'No, I suppose not,' I said. 'So which of the gods did Selene love?'

'She didn't love a god at all, my dear. In fact, Selene's one true love was Endymion, a mortal prince.'

I was intrigued. From the little I knew, liaisons between gods and mortals rarely ended well. 'Tell me more.'

'One day, whilst out hunting on Mount Latmus, Prince Endymion decided to rest and subsequently fell asleep in a woodland grotto. Soon, darkness fell and Selene, the Moon Goddess, rose in the sky. As She journeyed across the heavens, Her light fell upon the face of the sleeping Endymion, and She was immediately captivated by his beauty.'

'Oh, how romantic,' I sighed.

'Indeed it was, and each night as Selene rose, She gazed upon the handsome prince, and each night She fell just a little more in love with him. Understanding however, that as a mortal, he would age and die, She decided to approach Zeus and ask Him to grant Endymion immortality so that She would never lose him.'

'And He agreed?' I asked. 'I would have thought that given Her and Zeus' past relationship, He wouldn't have looked too kindly upon Her taking another lover.'

Mrs Darley smiled. 'And you are quite right, my dear, for although Zeus agreed, He did impose a certain condition upon Selene's request.'

'That doesn't surprise me.'

'He consented on condition that Endymion would, from that point on, always remain asleep and never again look upon Selene's face.'

'Oh, that's so sad,' I said, 'and did She agree?'

'She did. She thought it more bearable to gaze upon Endymion's face each night, rather than lose him completely. So, night after night, Selene continues to watch, not only over Her sleeping lover, but over us all as we sleep, caressing our dreams with enchanted images.'

'What a lovely story,' I said, 'sad in some ways, but beautiful in others.'

'I hope you don't mind me saying this, my dear,' said Mrs Darley, 'but in a way it reminds me of you.'

'Me?' I asked, 'in what way?'

'Your lovers also seem to be asleep,' she said gently.

I looked down, embarrassed to meet her gaze, and felt the colour rush to my cheeks.

'I'm fine the way I am,' I said defensively.

'But we all need love my dear, and somehow, I think you prevent it from entering your life. Just like Selene, you look and dream, but you do not participate.'

My cheeks continued to burn.

'I'm not trying to pry or interfere,' she said, 'but sometimes work can take over your life, making joy and pleasure a distant memory. Perhaps, as we approach the first quarter Moon, when She is half in light and half in shadow, you might consider using Her powers to bring a little balance into your life. You deserve it, and the goddess insists upon it.'

I could not hide my surprise. 'Does She?'

Mrs Darley smiled. 'Oh yes.'

She turned away and concentrated her gaze upon the fire, the flames of which leapt and danced in the candlelight. Presently, she began to speak the most beautiful words that touched my soul.

'Listen to the words of the Great Goddess, She, who of old was also called among men, Isis, Astarte, Diana, Ge, Aphrodite, Melusine, Luna, Morgan, Brigid, Freyja, Arianrhod, Danu, and by many other names.

'Whenever you have need of anything, once in the month, and better it be if the Moon is full, then shall you gather in some secret place, and worship the spirit of me, for I am the great Goddess. Beneath the Moon shall you assemble, you who wish to learn all mysteries but have not yet won its deepest secrets. To these shall I teach things as yet unknown, and you shall be free from slavery, and as a sign that you be truly free, you shall be naked in your rites, and you shall dance, sing, feast, make music and love, all in my praise. For mine is the ecstasy of the spirit, and mine is also joy upon earth, for my law is love unto all things.'

'Oh my goodness, that is so beautiful,' I said. 'What is it?'

'It's just a small part of something called, *The Charge of the Goddess.*'

'I've never heard of it. I'm sorry.'

'Don't be sorry my dear, there's no reason you should have heard of it unless you've moved in Wiccan or witchcraft circles.'

I sat, not really knowing what to say. The word 'witchcraft' filled me with fear, and the word 'Wicca' I didn't understand, but how could something that was supposedly so evil, produce words that were so beautiful?

'The Charge,' continued Mrs Darley, 'is probably one of the most famous pieces of prose in modern witchcraft, and has its roots in Charles Leyland's book, *Aradia, The Gospel of Witches.* It is however, to Doreen Valiente, the renowned mid twentieth century witch, that we are indebted for it becoming the beautiful piece of prose I have just quoted to you.'

'Well, it is very lovely,' I said, wishing I could recall it fully, and wondering if my neighbour might repeat it so that I might write it down.

'Perhaps it might be something you wish to become more familiar with in the future, my dear, but just for now, drink in the words and ponder on their meaning,' she said, as she once again repeated the final part.

'And so, you shall dance, sing, feast, make music and love, all in my praise. For mine is the ecstasy of the spirit, and mine is also joy upon earth, for my law is love unto all things.'

To my surprise, I suddenly became aware of hot, burning tears blurring my vision, and quite against my will, they made a bid for freedom, spilling down my cheeks and falling gently into my wine.

'Ah,' said Mrs Darley, her voice filled with compassion, 'at last, my Moon child shows some emotion, and allows herself to consider the possibility of becoming liberated from her self- imposed cell of imprisonment.'
She leaned forward and touched her glass to mine. 'May Selene bring you a love of freedom, and the freedom to love, my dear,' she said.

I always fancy that it is not only humankind who are entranced by the light of the Moon, but that other levels of existence are also moved by Her unrivalled beauty and the potential for weaving magick. This poem is in honour of those who live at the edge of our imagination.

Moon Fae

Lifting the darkness,
Her silvered light bathes the land,
Rousing it
From dreamless slumber.

On gossamer wings,
Wet still, from birthing waters
They rise.
To live, to dance, to die beneath her gaze.

Chapter Seven

New Moon Magick

Akin to new beginnings, the waxing new Moon hangs like a silver crescent against the early evening sky, between one to three days after Her inception. This phase of the Moon is full of promise, hence new Moon magick is dedicated to planning new projects, visualising desires and preparing for action. Her reappearance in the night sky encourages hope, and instils within us the belief that our deepest wishes can manifest, if we are willing to take our magick seriously.

This Moon equates to the Maiden (or Son for men), although the term 'Maiden' does not necessarily mean virginal or chaste, but rather a young lady who is wild, free, and spirited. She may also be a powerful warrior, yet will always retain her femininity, and she is just discovering her sexuality, yet will not be owned by any man. The Maiden Goddess is represented in many forms throughout the world, although the Greek goddess Artemis probably captures the spirit of the archetypal Maiden.

Artemis was the Goddess of the chase, forests, sudden death, childbirth, and the Moon (although Selene eventually replaced Her in the latter role). Various claims were made for Her parentage, ranging from the union of Zeus and Demeter, to Dionysus and Isis, although the Greeks usually portrayed Her as the daughter of Zeus and Leto, and twin sister to Apollo.

Legend tells us that as soon as She was born, Artemis went to Her father and asked for his permission that She might always remain chaste, rather than be promised to any man. Zeus, perhaps rather surprisingly, given his own penchant for romantic relationships of all kinds, agreed to his daughter's request. Artemis then went on to ask if She might be clad in a short hunting tunic and boots, which She regarded as the perfect attire for the Goddess of the Chase, and once again Zeus adhered to Her wishes.

Artemis then chose to live an austere outdoor life, where there was little room for affairs of the heart, for She considered both marriage and love-making repugnant. In fact, Artemis was one of the few deities over whom Aphrodite, the Goddess of love, had little power.

Artemis was followed and venerated by many young Maidens, all of whom were required to make a vow of chastity which, if broken, carried severe penalties. If any of Artemis' followers wished to marry, they would be required to sacrifice their hair to Her.

It wasn't however, only the maidens of Artemis who felt Her wrath. One day, whilst bathing in the river Parthenius, Artemis was spotted by the young and handsome hunter, Actaeon, who, captivated by Her naked beauty and raw power, leaned against a tree to watch at Her. Unfortunately for Actaeon, Artemis saw him looking, and feeling that Her privacy had been violated, immediately turned him into a stag. Not satisfied with this act of retribution however, She then set Actaeon's own hunting dogs upon him, and watched as they tore him apart.

This story of Artemis illustrates that despite Her often, gentle portrayal as a Maiden, She can, at times, be both powerful and ruthless, traits that are particularly noticeable when She feels She is being disrespected, or desired purely for Her physical beauty. This Goddess stands by Her principles whatever the cost. She is both protective and fiercely independent, whilst still retaining the impetuosity of youth. Call upon Her whenever self-assurance is required, or the ability to stand on your own two feet.

For those who have youth on their side, the Maiden is easy to relate to. She is of course beautiful, has firm, flawless skin, a waist that many, who are past the first flush of youth, can only dream of, and that enviable attitude where she believes anything is possible. The Maiden often has an infectious charm, an impetuosity that makes the pulse quicken and the heart sing. She brings joy and the whisper of endless possibilities on the crescent of a new Moon.

In reality however, young women are often under tremendous stress in our modern society. They have to cope with puberty and the onset of menstruation, deal with the pressures of education and exams, and the expectations (often of others) to get a job, or carve out a successful career. This is of course, all in addition to giving thought to how they feel about their physical appearance, and the prospect of attracting a sexual partner. The media applies relentless pressure, urging them to seek physical perfection, at any cost. These new and exciting experiences can often lead to early burn out, where young women become anxious, depressed, and unable to relax.

On the other hand, those in the Mother and Wise Woman stages of life, should never abandon the call of the Maiden, for she resides in us all, just waiting for the chance to be invited out to play. In fact, those who are about to become Wise Women, often find that the Maiden bubbles irrepressibly to the surface and that they have more time to get to know her better than they perhaps did when they were young.

The following meditation should prove invaluable to Maidens of any age, regardless of whether they are just about to forge their way in the world, or begin a new chapter in their lives.

New Moon, Maiden Meditation:

Sit quietly, somewhere you will not be disturbed. Put on some music, burn incense or essential oils of your choice (fresh aromas such as Lemon, Lemongrass, Bergamot, Orange, Mandarin and Jasmine are particularly recommended for invoking Maiden energies), and become aware of your breathing. Don't try to alter it in any way, but simply become aware of its gentle rhythm, as you breathe in and out... in and out.

Now imagine that you have stepped out into a warm summer's evening. Dusk is about to fall, and the slender crescent of a new Moon smiles down, full of promise, full of hope.

The grass feels soft beneath your feet, and as you look around, you become aware that you are standing at the foot of a magnificent tor. The tor rises high above you, and you are filled with a desire to climb to the summit, to look out over what you know will be an enchanted landscape. In this moment, you are filled with the spirit of the Maiden, and you can feel that youthful exuberance calling you to adventure.

You stand, looking at the tor in the soft blue haze of twilight, noticing there are several paths leading up towards the summit. Some rise steeply and lead straight to the top without wavering, some zig zag sharply from side to side, whilst others seemingly disappear and reappear as they wind gently around the hillside.

As you stare at the paths before you, you become aware that each one represents a different way of approaching a current challenge or decision in your life. You look at the paths which appear silver in the moonlight and suddenly become aware of a beautiful young woman walking down the hill towards you. As She comes closer, you notice that

Her pale blue gown has an almost luminous quality to it, and you instinctively know that this is the Maiden Moon Goddess, She to whom you can turn for advice as to which path you should choose.

The Goddess stops just in front of you and smiles and Her kindly radiance makes you feel that She understands your hesitancy. She gently points out that each path has its advantages and each, its challenges. Some paths offer a direct route to your destination, but will be tiring and demanding. Some will lead in many different directions, taking you on a sometimes frustrating, yet interesting journey, whilst others may take much longer, but will provide a gentler, meandering route.

Take a moment now in the company of the Maiden Moon Goddess, seizing the opportunity to talk to Her about your dreams and aspirations, and allow Her to lead you along the route that is best suited to the next stage of your journey. Only when you feel ready, should you begin your ascent along your chosen path.

***

Now, having finally reach the summit of the tor, you take a moment to enjoy a quiet sense of achievement, and as you look around, you notice that the Maiden Moon goddess is once again waiting for you. She indicates that you take time to savour this moment, to sit, to be still, and to look out over the enchanted landscape that unfolds below you.

***

Now the Maiden goddess places Her hand on your arm, and you feel it radiating with warmth and light. In this rare moment of peace and stillness, you begin to understand that regardless of the path you take in life, you will always be brought to where you need to be. Sometimes it may take longer, sometimes it may be more challenging, sometimes you will feel as though you're simply going backwards and forwards, but always, *always,* you will reach your destination.

With this insight, you turn to thank Her, but the lady in the luminous blue gown is no longer beside you, and for the briefest of moments you feel saddened. But then, you look up and there, against the backdrop of the evening sky, the Maiden Moon Goddess smiles down, and shines Her pale new light upon your chosen path.

Within moments you find yourself once again standing at the base of the tor, and in your own time, with the wisdom of the Maiden Moon Goddess in your heart, you gradually bring yourself back to the awareness of the present, and open your eyes.

New Moon Superstitions and Folklore

The new Moon is thought to be an auspicious time for:

- Beginning building projects
- Moving into a new home
- Getting married
- Checking your bank balance and investments
- Cutting hair and nails
- Cutting healing herbs
- Exercising

It is considered unlucky to see the new Moon for the first time in its cycle without having silver coins in your pocket, as they should immediately be turned over in order to secure an increase in fortune during the month ahead. Alternatively, in certain areas (and for those who are physically flexible), luck will be yours if you perform a somersault in front of the crescent Moon.

In Devon, it is thought that the new Moon should only be looked at over the right shoulder, as looking at it over the left attracts bad luck. Elsewhere, people say that the Moon should only be looked at straight ahead, and that *any* turn of the head in order to view the new Moon will bring bad luck.

Likewise, to see the new Moon for the first time through the trees is considered unlucky, whilst to see it through glass indicates that glass will be broken before the month is out. Pointing at the Moon is also usually taboo.

Matters of love are also associated with the new Moon, and in Devon, young girls would go out under the light of the midsummer Moon, sit on a stile, turn their back upon it, and say:

> *'All hail, new moon, all hail to thee!*
> *I prithee, good moon, reveal to me*
> *This night who shall my true love be*
> *Who he is and what he wears,*
> *And what he does all months and years.'*

The day upon which the new Moon appears also seems to be of the utmost importance in folklore.

In Italy, Wednesday's new Moon is dreaded, as they believe that misfortune will follow, whilst in France, as in Britain, Fridays are considered inauspicious, as indicated by the following rhyme:

> *'Friday's moon,*
> *Come when it wull* (sic)
> *It comes too soon.'*

Saturday too seems to be an unpopular choice for the new Moon, as does Sunday for a full Moon:

> *'Saturday's new and Sunday's full,*
> *Never was good and never wull* (sic)*.'*

Whilst the following rhyme seems to sum up the disdain with which the Cornish once greeted a Saturday new Moon:

> *'A Saturday moon,*
> *If it comes once in seven years,*
> *Comes once too soon.'*

It is thought that the tradition of bowing, or curtseying to the Maiden or full Moon was a way of counteracting bad luck, and that this custom has its origins in Anglo Saxon times.

Robert Graves, the celebrated author, was so enamoured with the Moon that his children considered him rather an embarrassment, as he always acknowledged the new Moon's presence wherever he was, by bowing to it nine times.

In fact, Graves believed that the Moon's influence over the lives of every living creature on earth was unquestionable, and maintained that the Moon deity, which he named 'The White Goddess', contained a Divine source of energy. Graves also wrote a book entitled, *The White Goddess,* in which he expands his theories.

New Moon Celebrations and Rituals

A Moon celebration, regardless of its phase, can be as simple or as complex as you wish, depending on preference and/or experience.

If you are well versed in formal magickal practice and wish to cast a spell, then the casting of a circle, changing your consciousness, path-working and both feeling and visualising the outcome, will most probably form part of your Moon ritual.

If however, you just wish to acknowledge a particular Moon phase, then simply light a candle, burn incense or oils, play music of your choice, and perhaps use some of the suggestions given below to formulate your own Moon celebration.

A New Moon Altar

You may care to set up a small altar in your home or garden, and incorporate any of the following as decoration, or use ideas of your own.

- A dish, bowl or chalice of water to symbolise the pull of the tides
- White or silver candles
- A white altar cloth
- White Flowers
- Silver coins
- Shells
- Crescent shaped Moon
- A statue to represent the Maiden Goddess (Artemis, Bride, Persephone)

- Something to represent what you wish to achieve during this new cycle of the Moon.

Honouring the new Moon usually takes place within three days of its new phase, albeit, it is best to wait until She is visible in the sky (usually twenty-four to forty eight hours after Her birth), as this will make your celebration, ritual or spell work more effective. If it is possible, go outside and stand beneath Her, even if you then choose to practice your ritual indoors. Take a few moments in which to mediate on what this new Moon means to you, and what seeds you would like to sow, in order to bring your desires ever closer during the lunar cycle ahead. You may find it helpful to use the guided visualization above, or to simply meditate quietly.

New Moon Magick

The new Moon is all about sowing the seeds to initiate new beginnings, although it may take longer than one lunar cycle to bring those seeds to maturity. This is the time to allow ideas to germinate, to give a voice to your dreams, and allow their energy to spiral out into the world.

The following is a generic new Moon spell for growth, which can be moulded and shaped to suit various needs.

Seed Planting Spell

You will need:

- A jug of water (preferably rainwater, or fresh water from the sea, a river, lake or pool), that has been blessed by you beneath the light of the new crescent.

An example of such a blessing might be:

'Goddess of the Maiden Moon, please bless this water with your gentle energy that it might nourish all it touches.'

- A pot of soil
- Seeds of your choice (one to represent each idea/person/ relationship etc)

Casting your spell:

- Take time to be still and to engage the power of your mind, emotions and senses, to see, smell, taste, hear and feel your desired outcome. Then, holding that intent in the forefront of your mind, plant your seed(s) in the pot of soil.
- Water the seeds and perhaps say a few words as a blessing over them. You can adapt the blessing below, the water blessing above, or better still, write your own.
- Tend your seeds carefully, for they are symbolic of your dreams becoming reality, and as you do so, go out into the world and act in accord, doing whatever you can on the physical plane, to bring about your desires.

New Moon Blessing

Lady of the crescent Moon,
Whose arms hold the dark orb of potential,
Shine on my dreams
That they too, may wax with your light.

Toasting the New Moon

You may wish to raise a toast to the Moon, to acknowledge Her presence, or simply to give thanks. Drinks such as elderflower cordial, apple juice, or white wine, each of which symbolise the pale light of the new crescent, are appropriate.

In addition, you might wish to eat something to ground yourself, especially if you have carried out a meditation or spell work. Croissants make a suitable new Moon food as they mirror the shape of the new crescent. Some magickal practitioners will take a little of the drink or food and offer it to the deities. If you are outside, it can be placed directly onto the Earth, whilst if you are inside, it can be placed in a bowl, and offered to the Earth following your ritual.

We each carry the Maiden (or the Son) inside us, regardless of our age. She is that part that throws caution to the wind and dances in the moonlight, or on a windswept shore, but she is also that part that will not be taken advantage of and who wishes to make her mark on the world.

She is an aspect of our psyche that we should never lose, so, when the Maiden Moon next lights our skies with Her delicate beauty, stand for a moment beneath Her, drink deeply of Her presence to imbibe the spirit, and feel the impetuosity of youth calling you to adventure.

Mrs Darley Tale: What Might Be

The granite steps sparkled in the light of the full Moon as I opened the door of Mrs Darley's cottage.

'Thank you for a wonderful evening,' I said, turning to give my hostess a hug. 'What a lovely way to celebrate both the Winter Solstice and the full Oak Moon.'

'I'm glad you enjoyed it my dear,' said Mrs Darley, 'but watch how you go down those steps, they look very icy. I really must get someone round to put a handrail up.'

'I'll be fine,' I said, gingerly negotiating the top two steps before reaching out and seizing the welcome trunk of a substantial wisteria bush as I reached the bottom of the steps.

'Oh wait a second,' said Mrs Darley, returning indoors for a moment and then reappearing, 'I almost forgot... I meant to give you this.'

She waved a small object in the air, before dropping it into my outstretched hand. I looked down and saw that it was a red silk bag secured by a drawstring tied in a bow.

'Shall I open it now?' I asked looking up at her, whilst wondering whether I would be able to see it by moonlight.

She nodded, 'Why not? Look upon it as a congratulatory gift, in recognition of getting your promotion.'

'Thank you,' I said, carefully untying the bow and tipping out what felt like a piece of rock onto my hand. I suddenly gasped in delight as the moonlight caught the stone and for the briefest of moments, it was almost as though I held a pool of milk in the palm of my hand.

'It's beautiful. What is it?'

'A Moonstone,' said Mrs Darley.

'The only Moonstone I've ever heard of is the one at the top of the copse, where we celebrated the lunar eclipse,' I said.

Mrs Darley smiled. 'Well, it's certainly not from there.'

'What is it used for?'

'Protecting travellers.'

'I wasn't intending to go anywhere,' I laughed, 'unless you know different?'

'The future is never set in stone my dear, if you'll forgive the pun, but occasionally we are given just a glimpse of what it could be.'

I looked at her, not knowing whether I was ready to hear what she had to say.

'Tonight,' she said, 'when we were all having a bit of fun, seeing what the future would hold as we each roasted a chestnut on the fire, I watched yours positively jump and dance out across the hearth.'

I remembered only too well. It had made me jump, but I had just put it down to there being too much moisture in the nut.

'Well, yes, I know it was a bit animated, but surely you can't predict my future simply based on the fact that I happened to choose a rather damp chestnut?'

Mrs Darley laughed. 'Put like that my dear, it does sound quite preposterous, but someone I once knew and was very fond of, placed much store in chestnut divining.'

'But I have no intention of going anywhere,' I said, trying to ignore the cold hand of fear that had momentarily touched my heart. 'I love it here.'

'I'm sure you do, and I'm not saying that this adventure is imminent, I only said it was a probability. Sometimes my dear, our life mission demands that we break free from the safe cocoon we build around ourselves and eventually, we are compelled to go wherever it leads.'

'But where would I go, and why?'

'That's not for me to say,' said Mrs Darley, gently. 'Look, I didn't mean to alarm you, and you're right, you probably just had an overactive chestnut due to it having a high moisture content. And of course, don't forget that this new job will involve plenty of travelling around.'

I nodded, but in my heart knew that she had only mentioned the travelling aspect of my job as an attempt to placate me. It hadn't worked however, and my peace of mind was ruffled.

Nevertheless, I turned and managed a smile as I stepped down onto the path.

'Thank you,' I said, 'both for the evening and for the Moonstone, they were, and are, much appreciated.'

I felt her watching me as I put the key in my front door.

'Keep the Moonstone close, my dear,' she called, 'for it is also a companion to the traveller who seeks the mysteries of life.'

This poem was inspired by the ancients and their lack of understanding as to why the Moon disappeared for three nights each month. This led them to feel almost abandoned by Her as She slipped into the darkness, wondering if She would ever return to light the night skies. This is the Moon's reply to their fears.

Rebirth

Do not mourn,
As the darkness claims my light.
Do not weep
For that which fades
And once shone so bright.

Do not grieve,
As my Moon tides ebb and wane,
For I shall rise
And so your eyes
Shall meet my gaze again.

Chapter Eight

Waxing Moon Magick

As the new crescent Moon waxes, so Her light shines ever brighter. A week after Her birth, at the first quarter phase, She is half in darkness and half in light, beautifully balanced between the poles of opposites, and this is the perfect time to bring balance into our lives. As Her light continues to grow and She moves into the waxing gibbous phase, it is time to give impetus to everything we began at the new Moon.

The waxing Moon is the Enchantress (or Warrior for men), for She exudes confidence as She stamps Her independence on the night sky, and calls us to mirror Her example. She beckons us to move forward, to take action and not allow ourselves to be held back, or be prevented from achieving our desired goals and dreams.

Waxing Moon magic pushes us to make the phone call, apply for the job, ask the new neighbours round to dinner, book the weekend away, or ask that special someone out. She says *carpe diem* (seize the day) and live in the moment.

Aphrodite, the Greek Moon Goddess and also the Goddess of Love, captures the essence of the Enchantress as the Maiden comes of age. Fair and beautiful, Aphrodite, presides over all acts of love and pleasure. Her name means 'born of the foam', as She was conceived within the foaming waves of the ocean by the semen of Uranus, the God of Heaven, when his genitals fell into the sea, having been castrated upon his wife's orders by his son, Chronos.

Carried along on the breath of the west wind, Zephyrus,

Aphrodite finally arrived on the shores of Cyprus. Here, She was greeted by the Horae, who were the Goddesses of the Seasons and the natural order of things, who dressed Her in beautiful clothes, adorned Her with jewels, and led Her to the assembly of the immortals.

The gods were immediately struck by Aphrodite's seductive beauty, witty conversation, gracious laughter, sweet deceits, and all the charms and delights of love.

Of all the gods on Olympus however, it was Hephaestus, the ugly and unpolished blacksmith deity, who won Aphrodite as his wife. Zeus was happy to bless the union, as Hephaestus had earlier released Hera (Zeus' wife), from a magickal trap. Zeus also saw this marriage as a way of quashing the amorous attentions of other would-be suitors, who wished to possess this enchanting Goddess of beauty.

The marriage of Hephaestus and Aphrodite however, was not a happy one, and despite Zeus' hopes, Aphrodite was never short of admirers to distract Her from her marital bed, including Ares, Hermes, and even Zeus himself. Among Her many conquests however, there were two lovers who held a special place in Her heart, Anchises the Trojan, and Adonis.

Aphrodite first noticed Anchises, whilst he was tending his flock on Mount Ida. Having anointed Her body with scented oils, and adorned Herself with jewels, Aphrodite approached Anchises and told him that She was the daughter of Otreus, King of Phrygia, and that Her only desire was to become his wife. Overwhelmed by Aphrodite's beauty, Anchises was only too willing to make love to Her, but when he awoke sometime later, he was horrified to see the Goddess Aphrodite standing before him, in all her immortal splendour.

Anchises was understandably filled with terror, for any mortal who slept with a deity was usually punished with premature aging and death. Aphrodite however, reassured him that all would be well, and that She would give him a son who would be like a god. There was however one condition: Anchises had to swear never to reveal the true identity of the child's mother. He immediately agreed to Her request, and the child became Aeneas, a wise and well-respected warrior, who according to the *Aeneid*, would later escape from the ruins of Troy with his father Anchises, and young son, Ascanius.

Aphrodite's other great love was the handsome Adonis, God of Beauty and Desire. Legend has it that Adonis was conceived after his mother, Myrrha, tricked her own father, Theias, king of Syria, to sleep with her. So horrified was the king when he discovered that his lover was in fact his daughter, that he swore to hunt her down and kill her. Myrrha, meanwhile, in fear of her life, begged the gods to save her, and was immediately transformed into a Myrrh tree, from which Adonis was born.

One day, whilst walking past the Myrrh tree, Aphrodite noticed the new-born child, and as She picked him up, She was immediately bewitched by his beauty. Concerned for his safety however, She placed him in a coffer, and asked Persephone, Queen of the Underworld, to attend to his upbringing. When Aphrodite later came to claim him, She found that Persephone, too, had become dazzled by the young Adonis, and refused to part with him.

The two Goddesses then fell into a heated dispute as to who should win the handsome God, and the matter was finally brought before Zeus. He ruled that Adonis should spend a third of the year with Persephone in the Underworld, a third with Aphrodite in the realm of the gods, and a third with whomsoever he chose – his choice was Aphrodite.

Aphrodite illustrates through these powerful stories, how

the Enchantress often attains her desires through the use of her feminine wiles, albeit not always in a sexual manner, but through her charm, eloquence, and compassion.

The age of the Enchantress is an exciting one. This is when the Maiden reaches maturity, and can enjoy all the gifts of her femininity, including intimate relationships, regardless of her sexual preferences. She begins to grow into a confident young woman, with a sense of who she is now that the trauma of puberty is past. This is when she is often called upon to make choices, many of which offer her the opportunity to engage with the wild adventure of life, before duty and responsibility beckon.

Occasionally however, she is faced with difficult decisions. Should she choose a career that requires her to stay in the place she knows, with family and friends around her, or to travel and take a job which requires her to move and leave all that is familiar? Should she commit to a particular relationship, or remain free to meet and have relationships with whosoever she chooses?

The age of choices can often be overwhelming and the meditation below may help to prioritise those which are important at this exciting stage of life.

Waxing Moon Enchantress Meditation

Sit quietly, somewhere you will not be disturbed. Play music, burn incense or oils of your choice (those which open the heart chakra are particularly recommended for invoking enchantress energies. These include Jasmine, Neroli, Ginger, Patchouli and Ylang Ylang), and just become aware of your breathing. Don't try to alter it in any way, but just pay attention to its gentle rhythm, as you breathe in and out... in and out.

Now imagine that you have stepped out, barefooted

beneath the light of a first quarter waxing Moon, and as you look around, you find yourself standing on a white desert island beach. The heat of the day remains in the sand as you begin to walk towards the water's edge. There is hardly a ripple on the sea and the Moon shines on the water, transforming it into a silver mirror.

As you walk along, you suddenly become aware of something hard beneath your feet. You bend down and begin to brush the sand away with your hands. You feel a surge of excitement as you appear to uncover what looks like the curved lid of a box, the metal clasps of which shine in the moonlight, and you eagerly begin to scoop out the sand around the box.

Suddenly the box becomes loose and you drag it out, setting it down carefully upon the beach. As you dust off the remaining grains of sand, you begin to think that perhaps this is no ordinary box, for it seems to resemble a treasure chest and suddenly, feeling full of anticipation, you carefully release the clasps and throw back the lid.

The contents are captivating, for here, bathed in the light of the Moon and sitting on a dark velvet cushion, are seven crystals, whilst on the inside of the lid, a rhyme is written:

> *'Within this chest once lost and once drowned,*
> *A glimpse of your future now can be found.*
> *Beneath the moon's light you'll seek and you'll find*
> *The stone that speaks to heart, body and mind'.*

You look at the stones laid out before you as they shimmer and gleam beneath the light of the Moon: a red garnet, an orange carnelian, a yellow amber, a green malachite, a deep blue lapis, a violet iolite, and a clear quartz crystal all vie for your attention. You instinctively know that you have not happened upon this treasure chest by accident, and that one of these stones has a message for you. Take a moment to look at each one, to run your hands across them and to feel their energies.

Perhaps the red garnet may have a message about the direction your life is taking, or somehow gives you permission to release thought patterns and ideas that were once appropriate, but which you have long since outgrown. The orange carnelian may inspire you to put your creative forces to good use, or to look at the reasons behind some of your relationships – reminding you to always honour yourself. The yellow amber may fill you with strength and self-confidence, to enable you to make a move you've always dreamed of, whether this is in the realms of travel, career, or other life choices.

The green malachite speaks of affairs of the heart – this may be concerning relationships with lovers, family or friends, or it may be more about learning to release negative and destructive emotions. The deep blue lapis is a physical and emotional healing stone, that also gives you permission and the voice to speak your truth, and to forge your own way, regardless of what others may think. The violet iolite can assist with the opening of the third eye, to help you to attune to that deeper, intuitive part of your soul.

Finally, the clear quartz crystal asks you to step back and look at the bigger picture. It asks you to appreciate and realise your value here on this Earth plane and leads you to understand how you can contribute to this fascinating web of life. It can also help you to connect with your own particular spiritual path, or to cultivate a relationship with divinity, whatever, or whoever, you perceive that to be.

Be still now for a moment, choose your stone, hold it in your hand, and listen to the message held within.

***

Now, with that message stored within your heart and mind, you carefully place the crystal back in the box, close the lid, and fasten the clasps. You rise to your feet and notice that the incoming tide is almost within reach, and so, you leave the chest to await its fate, as it is once more washed away by the sea to new shores, where someone else is destined to receive a message from the stones.

Soon now it will be time to leave this beautiful island, so, as the water begins to lap gently around the treasure chest, look up once more into the night sky, and give thanks to the waxing Moon – The Enchantress – for shining Her light on the treasure you have been privy to and for imparting a little of Her wisdom through the medium of the stones.

Now, whenever you are ready, bring yourself back to the awareness of the present, and gradually open your eyes.

Waxing Moon Superstitions and Folklore

- Bacon yield from a pig will be more.
- If Christmas day falls on a waxing Moon, then the following year will be a lucky one.

Waxing Moon Celebrations and Rituals

Moon celebrations, regardless of their phase, can be as simple, or as complex as you wish, depending on preference and/or experience. If you are well versed in formal magickal practice and wish to cast a spell, then the casting of a circle, changing your consciousness, path working, and both feeling and visualising the outcome, will most probably form part of your Moon ritual.

If however, you just wish to acknowledge a particular Moon phase, then simply light a candle, burn incense or oils, play music of your choice, and perhaps use some of the suggestions given below to formulate your own Moon celebration.

A Waxing Moon Altar

You may care to set up a small altar in your home or garden, and incorporate any of the following, either as decoration, or use ideas of your own.

- A dish, bowl or chalice of water, to represent the pull of the tides
- Black and white candles
- A white altar cloth
- A yin and yang symbol, to represent the light and dark aspects of the Moon
- Contrasting colours of flowers can represent both halves of the Moon – purple and yellow, deep blue and orange, or red and white
- Silver coins
- Shells
- A statue to represent any of the goddesses of enchantment, such as Aphrodite, Venus, Rhiannon
- Something that symbolises what you are attempting to bring into your life as the Moon begins to wax. For example, if you planted seeds at the new Moon, then you might like to place these on your altar, especially if they have begun to germinate.

Honouring the waxing Moon can take place anytime between four and twelve days after the birth of the new Moon, according to the changes you wish to manifest in your life. If possible, go outside and stand beneath Her, even if you choose to practice your ritual indoors.

Take a few moments in which to mediate on what this waxing Moon means to you. Perhaps you wish to bring balance into your life, as the first quarter phase comes into being, a week after the birth of the new Moon? If so, you may like to light black and white candles, to represent the light and dark halves of the Moon, or to hold a yin and yang symbol, symbolising harmony and balance.

Or perhaps you are ready to take action now and bring the seeds you sowed at the new phase of the lunar cycle to fruition? If so, then honour the Moon during Her waxing gibbous phase, as She moves towards Her full light, eight to twelve days into the lunar cycle. Visualise clearly what you would like to bring into your life as the energies begin to quicken. You may find it helpful to use the guided visualization above, or to simply meditate quietly.

Waxing Moon Magick

The waxing moon can be about bringing balance into your life, or moving projects forward, both of which often need strength, courage, and a boost of positivity.

What follows is a simple and delicious generic waxing Moon spell, that can be moulded and shaped to suit your needs:

Spicy Cup Cake Spell

You will need:

- A cupcake or fairy cake, flavoured with cinnamon and/or ginger (see recipe below). Alternatively, make a cup of ginger root tisane, with a pinch of cinnamon as this too, will be equally as effective.

- A small dish.

Cup Cake Ingredients (Makes 12):

- 125g unsalted butter, softened
- 125g caster sugar
- 125g self-raising flour
- Pinch of salt
- Pinch of Cinnamon and /or ground ginger
- 2 medium eggs
- 2 tablespoons milk
- 1 x 12-hole muffin tin, lined with paper cases

Method:

- Set the oven to 190C, gas 5.
- Place the butter in a bowl and beat until soft.
- Add the sugar, flour, salt, eggs, cinnamon and/or ginger and milk, whisking until the mixture is smooth.
- Spoon, the mixture equally into the paper cases.
- Bake for 15 - 18 minutes, until the cupcakes are a light golden colour.

- Remove from the oven. Leave the cupcakes to cool in the tin for a few minutes, before transferring them to a wire rack to cool.
- Decorate as you wish.

Casting your spell:

Take time to be still and engage the power of your mind, emotions, and senses, so that you will find the strength, courage, and positive energy to drive your goal forward. Then, holding that intent in the forefront of your mind, bless the cake. You could adapt the blessing below, use the following simple blessing, or better still, say one of your own.

'May my endeavours, just like this cake, rise and be blessed by the waxing Moon'.

Break off two pieces of the cake, offering the first piece to your deities, or the Earth if you prefer. If you are working outside, this may be placed directly upon the Earth itself, whilst if you are working inside, place your offering in a bowl, and empty it out onto the Earth following the completion of your ritual.

Eat the second piece of cake yourself, whilst visualising the strength of the ginger and cinnamon helping you to bring your goals into being.

Now go out into the world and act in accord on the physical plane to bring your desires to fruition.

Waxing Moon Blessing

Lady of the Waxing Moon,
Whose increasing light
Lifts the cloak of darkness,
Shine on my life, so that my strength/courage/self-belief might also grow.

Toasting the Waxing Moon

You may wish to raise a toast to the waxing Moon, to simply acknowledge Her presence, or to give thanks. As with the new Moon, white wine, elderflower cordial, or apple juice, are all appropriate drinks with which to honour the growing light of the Moon.

If you are not performing the act of magick suggested above, then you may wish to partake of some food in order to ground yourself, especially if you have carried out a meditation, or other form of spell work. A marbled cake, or a combination of white and brown bread, make suitable waxing moon food, as they represent the dark and light sides of the Moon. Golden foods, such as corn bread or honey cakes, represent Her growing light, and are also appropriate.

We all have the Enchantress (or the Warrior) within, even though we may have suppressed Her, due to society's expectations, or perhaps our own inhibitions. The Enchantress teaches us to be free, to cast off the worries of adolescence and pursue the life we came here to live before the responsibilities of the Mother (whether we have children or not), fall upon us. Regardless of our life stage or life phase, never lose touch with the Enchantress, for she can open doors that can otherwise only be dreamed of.

Mrs Darley Tale: The Hare in the Moon

'Once upon a time…' the unmistakable voice of Mrs Darley drifted into my dreams, and brought me back to the reality of a late afternoon in early summer, where the drone of the bees, and the sweet scent of roses, had lulled me into blissful slumber.

'The Buddha was wandering alone through a wood,' she continued, 'when he met a hare walking towards him, who asked him how he was.'

Fascinated, yet fully aware that I was eavesdropping from my well-hidden position behind the dry stonewall in my garden, I sat upright on the lounger and listened. My neighbour was telling a story, and I always loved to hear her tales.

'"I am cold and hungry," replied the Buddha.

'"I am sorry to hear that," said the hare. "Why don't you collect some sticks to make a fire, and I will find you some food?"

'The Buddha thanked the hare and began to set about finding sticks and lighting a fire. When the fire was blazing, the Buddha sat and waited, wondering what the hare would bring along to put in the pot. After a while, the hare returned, but to the Buddha's disappointment, appeared to be without any food. Nevertheless, the hare set a pot containing water upon the flames, and waited until it began to boil and then…,' Mrs Darley paused briefly for dramatic effect. 'Without a word, the hare jumped into the pot, offering his life so that the Buddha would not starve.'

I smiled at this rather moving story, and couldn't help wondering who was there with Mrs Darley out in the garden.

She continued, 'The Buddha, so grateful for the hare's actions, immediately plucked him from the pot, and set him in the Moon as an example of his selflessness and as an expression of the Buddha's thanks.'

'Is he still there?' The sound of a young boy's voice, clear and curious, took me by surprise.

'Why of course,' said Mrs Darley, 'and later this evening, before you go to bed, we will look for him.'

Delighted by what I had heard, but deciding that I had eavesdropped for long enough, I left the garden and made my way indoors.

***

Sitting down later that evening with a good book, I was aware of a timid knock on the window of the inner porch door, and upon investigating, I saw a young boy of around nine or ten, with gold rimmed glasses and tousled fair hair, standing in the porch whilst nervously fidgeting. I opened the door and smiled.

'Hello', I said, suspecting that this must be the young boy whose voice I had heard earlier in Mrs Darley's garden. 'How can I help you?'

His words came out in a somewhat nervous rush. 'Nanna sent me round to ask if you'd like to come and look for the hare in the Moon that the Buddha put there before I go to bed.'

In that moment I couldn't think of anything I would like better. 'I would love to,' I said, 'but first of all, tell me your name.'

'I'm Rowan, the same name as the tree in Nanna's garden. I'll tell her you're coming,' he said, and quickly ran back towards Mrs Darley's cottage, whilst I was left feeling as though I had been visited by a rather small, but amiable whirlwind.

I seemed to recall Mrs Darley telling me during one of

our many celebrations that the Rowan tree in her garden had been planted as a token of thanks for the safe delivery of her grandson, who apparently lived over on the Norfolk coast. She mentioned that she didn't get to see him very often, but suddenly here he was, and we were about to look for hares in the Moon together.

'Oh hello, dear.' Mrs Darley was leaning on the half stable door as I approached the steps. 'Do come in, I hope we haven't disturbed your evening, but earlier today, Rowan and I were talking about the Moon and whether anyone, or anything, actually lived on it. I told him that a hare lives there and that tonight we would try and see him under the waxing Moon, so we thought you might be interested to come and look for him too.'

'I would indeed,' I said, both fascinated and delighted to be part of this unexpected event. 'Thank you for asking me.'

'Well, you're just in time,' Mrs Darley nodded towards Dartmoor, 'the Moon's just coming up now. Rowan - come on - hurry up.' The boy came running from the direction of the kitchen, squeezing his way between us as Mrs Darley and I leaned over the half stable door, to witness the waxing gibbous Moon take Her place in the night sky.

'Where is she, Nanna?'

Mrs Darley pointed up at the Moon, and we all squinted, pondered, frowned, and debated. 'There look Rowan, can you make out the hare's ears, just there on the right?'

It took a few moments of intense concentration, but eventually we all agreed that there was indeed a hare looking down at us from his moonlit kingdom.

'Well, I think after all that hard work,' said Mrs Darley, turning away from the door, 'we deserve some light refreshments.'

As she disappeared into the kitchen, Rowan leaned

towards me, and whispered in rather a conspiratorial fashion, 'We've made hare cakes.'

For a brief moment I thought this sounded quite unappetising, until Mrs Darley came into the room with three steaming mugs of drinking chocolate and a plate of little fairy cakes sporting huge upright ears made of marzipan.

Much to Rowan's delight we all ate two cakes each and had a very serious discussion about the Moon being made of green cheese. It was such a profound experience to revisit the wonder of childhood with him, and Mrs Darley had so much patience, answering all his questions with her customary good humour and wisdom.

Eventually however, bedtime beckoned for Rowan, and upon her return from performing her grandmotherly duties, Mrs Darley poured us both a glass of whiskey, and we settled down by the fire.

'That was a lovely thing to do this evening,' I said. 'Rowan is such a delightful boy, and what's more, I had no idea that you could see a hare in the Moon.'

'Well, thank you for that my dear. I know I'm biased, but yes, Rowan *is* a lovely boy. He's quite quiet and sensitive, which are wonderful attributes, although I do worry that he might fall prey to those who have bullying tendencies.'

'Oh, I do hope not,' I said, remembering only too well from my own childhood, just how soul destroying it was to be bullied.

Mrs Darley smiled enigmatically. 'Don't worry, I shall do my best to surround him with protection. Anyway, my dear, with regards to your comment regarding hares in the Moon - one could write a whole book on the folklore of hares, and there is even a Moon called the Hare Moon.'

'I've never heard of the Hare Moon before,' I said, thoughtfully. 'When does it occur?'

'Our Celtic ancestors called the full Moon that fell in late April or early May, the Hare Moon and regarded the hare as being scared to the Goddess. Even Boudica, the leader of the Celtic Iceni tribe, is said to have carried a hare within her cloak, which she unleashed during her many battles with the Romans. She believed that the hare would bring her good fortune, and that the power of the Goddess would be with her.'

'Did it work?'

'For a while my dear, for a while. Indeed, she almost brought the Empire to its knees in Britain, but sadly, when she finally marched upon London, the might of the Roman army proved too much… still, who's to say that wasn't the will of the Goddess too?'

She left the question hanging in the air before continuing.

'Of course, many modern Pagans believe that the Saxon Goddess, Eostre, took the hare as her sacred animal, although there is no strong historical evidence for her existence. It does however make for a good story, and offers an attractive explanation as to how the hare became our familiar Easter bunny.'

I nodded. 'It is a good story,' I said, remembering how I had gone away and researched the story of Eostre and the hare, following our Spring Equinox celebrations the previous season.

'Mind you,' said Mrs Darley, 'in England, up until the nineteenth century, hares were thought to be the witch's familiar, and considered to be one of the animals into witches would metamorphose when they shape shifted under the light of the Moon.'

'Really?'

Mrs Darley nodded, whilst taking a sip of her whiskey. 'I remember reading a tale once, about a farmer whose cows wouldn't produce milk. So, being at the end of his tether, he went to visit a wise woman, and was told that his cows were being milked during the night, beneath the light of the Moon. The farmer of course was angry, and decided to lie in wait for the perpetrators the following evening.'

'Did he catch the them?' I asked.

'Yes, although not in the way he had expected. For this thief wasn't human, and the farmer watched in disbelief, as a brown hare ran into the cowshed, and began milking his cows. So, picking up his shotgun, the farmer followed the hare and shot her in the front paw with a silver sixpence.'

'Why a silver sixpence?'

'Well, silver is the sacred metal of the Moon, which probably explains why werewolves are also shot using a silver bullet. Anyway, to the farmer's surprise, milk began to pour from the gunshot wound on the hare's paw, and knowing she wouldn't be able to run very fast, the farmer followed her.

'Oh, don't tell me he caught her?' I asked.

'Well, as the hare reached the cottage of the old woman who lived right at the end of the village, she seemed to disappear. The farmer was determined to find out where the hare had gone, so he knocked on the door of the cottage until the old lady answered. He accused her of taking the hare into her cottage, which she most vehemently denied, but then the farmer noticed that the woman's hand was dressed in a fresh bandage. He immediately demanded that she undo the bandage, and when she did so, not only was it clear she had been wounded, but there in the centre of her palm was his silver sixpence.'

'What did he do?' I asked.

'He did what any God-fearing man would do, my dear,' laughed Mrs Darley, 'he ran off, terrified that he had just encountered a witch. But, from that day on, his cows always gave good milk.'

'So is seeing a hare really a bad omen?' I asked.

'Oh no,' said Mrs Darley emphatically, 'whenever we see a hare, we should feel blessed, for we may just have encountered the Moon Goddess, in one of Her many guises.'

The Moon, as Mrs Darley was very fond of pointing out, is most definitely a lady of illusion, and beneath Her beneficent gaze, many things change. Appearances are particularly softened in the moonlight, as the following poem illustrates.

Moon Alchemy

I watch you leave,
Your beauty unrivalled in the moonlight.
Soft, ageless, silvered.
Desire stirs,
For the one I have ceased to love
In the harsh light of day.

Chapter Nine

Full Moon Magick

The full Moon transforms everything She touches, and it is She who has the most profound effect on the psyche. She calls to witches, lovers, poets, and dreamers, beckoning them to create, and blossom beneath Her light, thereby reaching the pinnacle of their desires.

It is at this time that the seeds of hope, which were first dreamed of under the new crescent, and put into action beneath the cycle of the waxing Moon, come to fruition. Full Moon magic says, 'Now is the time'.

It is time to worship the gods, to go out on the first date, to throw the dinner party, to write the book. It is a time of action and high energy, a time to sing, dance, and make love, all beneath the blessing of the full Moon's light.

This Moon phase has become akin to the age of the Mother (or Protector for men). In this phase we acknowledge the Moon as the Mother Goddess, She who smiles down benevolently upon Her children, and whose borrowed light banishes the black abyss of night.

Our Moon Mother Goddess is Diana, Roman Goddess of the Hunt. She is a complex character, and it could be argued that She would just as easily be at home representing the Maiden Moon goddess, for She is often seen as the Roman counterpart of Artemis, due to Her association with hunting and chastity.

Diana was said to be the daughter of Jupiter and His mistress Latona, and was sister to the Sun God Apollo. It was She who superseded Luna, the original Roman Goddess of the Moon, and who was thought to have the ability to control the phases of the Moon from Her hunting chariot.

Regardless of Her associations with hunting and chastity however, Diana was also able to communicate with wild animals, and people also worshipped Her as a Goddess of children, childbirth, and fertility, just like Her Greek counterpart, Artemis. It was inevitable therefore, that She would be honoured amongst women.

In a similar fashion to the Moon, Diana could be unpredictable, and like Artemis, could also be vengeful, especially when men gazed upon Her merely as an object of desire. There is however, one myth that tells of a softer side to this Moon goddess.

Diana fell deeply in love with Orion, the giant huntsman, but Her brother Apollo was so horrified at the thought of his sister forming a relationship with a giant, that He constructed a plan to ensure that this would never happen.

Apollo, knowing only too well His sister's competitive nature, challenged Diana to a distance shooting contest. What Apollo didn't tell Diana, however, was that the shooting target was Orion's head, suitably disguised beneath a mask. Apollo knew without doubt, that Diana would hit Her target, due to Her prowess as a hunter. With the outcome of the contest assured, Diana therefore unknowingly killed Her prospective lover with Her own arrow. Horrified at Orion's death, the grieving Diana transformed him into a constellation and placed his hunting dogs, Canis Major, and Canis Minor, close by in the heavens.

Diana was also worshipped as the Goddess of the poorer members of society, and many plebeians and slaves received sanctuary in Her temples. This is also evidence of

Her compassionate, mothering nature, looking after those who were unable to stand up for themselves. It was said that even Her high priests were once slaves themselves.

Diana's festival was called *Nemoralia,* or the 'Festival of Torches', which was held on the 13th August. Her worshippers dressed their hair with flowers, and at dusk, would make their way to Lake Nemi, or 'Diana's Mirror' as it was fondly known, bearing torches that would reflect in the waters of the lake. On this day all hunting was forbidden, whilst also being a day of rest for both women and slaves.

Today, Diana is often referred to as the classic Mother Moon Goddess, She who depicts the dual qualities of strength and protection, both of which are an essential part of becoming the archetypal mother. The majority of us, regardless of our gender, or whether we have physically given birth or not, will experience this mothering instinct at some point in our lives, for we will all care for, or fight for, someone, or something we love.

Many modern-day Pagans also feel an irresistible draw to Diana, and still choose to celebrate Her feast day on 13th August, where offerings of bread and fruit are made, in return for Her blessings as darker times beckon.

Diana is, without doubt, a Mother Moon Goddess who is always in control, protecting Herself, and Her loved ones at any cost, and yet is also capable of showing a more benevolent side to Her nature, when the need arises.

The Mother age-group of today however, often find themselves under immense pressure trying to cope with all the demands of modern life, and Diana's methods are perhaps a mere ideal, which many attempt, but that few have any chance of attaining.

For those who are parents, juggling becomes the name of the game, from small children and nursery runs, to school children and extra-curricular activities.

Meanwhile, many women, both with and without children, are also trying to earn a living from part-time jobs to full-time careers, whilst at the same time attempting to give sufficient time to their family, their partner, their aged parents and their home and social life.

It is little wonder then, that this age group suffers from perhaps more stress than those of the Maiden, Enchantress, Wise Woman and Crone, as they often give up all their own needs and wants, in order to concentrate on those of others.

This may sound admirable, but everyone needs their own space and time to call their own, in the middle of a hectic and often chaotic lifestyle. The following meditation allows those who are experiencing the Mother stage of life, a chance to experience an oasis of calm.

Full Moon Mother Meditation

Sit quietly, somewhere you will not be disturbed. Play music, burn incense or oils of your choice (generous, abundant and balancing oils evocative of the Mother are all appropriate here, such as Rose, Geranium, Lavender and Clary Sage), and begin to become aware of your breathing, don't try to alter it in any way, but just become aware of its gentle rhythm, as you breathe in and out... in and out.

Now imagine you have stepped out onto a beautiful moonlit beach. The air is warm, the tide is out, and the silky sand appears silver in the light of the full Moon, feeling cool beneath your feet. You smell the saltiness of the sea as its aroma is carried to you on the evening breeze, and you can hear the soothing sound of the waves in the far distance.

You begin to walk across the soft sand, and as you near

the far side of the beach, the full light of the Moon highlights a cave carved deep into the rocks. Normally you would not venture in during the hours of darkness, but as you approach, you see that this cave appears to be softly lit by pale green lanterns, and you immediately feel drawn to enter.

Once inside, you follow a clearly marked path as it slopes gently downwards, before opening up into a beautiful dome-shaped chamber where, at the far end, you see a solitary candle burning upon a low altar.

As you stand before the altar, you suddenly become aware of the most beautiful haunting voices, women's voices - rising in song and reverberating round the cave, weaving a web of stillness and peace within you. You sink down into the soft, cool sand, where you immediately feel safe and secure, almost as though you are a child again, surrounded by loving energies.

***

As you sit, surrounded by this hypnotic web of sound, you begin to realise that this cave houses the chamber of the Mother. This is the sacred womb, from which all life springs, in which, all things are nurtured, nourished, and replenished, and you feel moved to connect with this loving energy.

Perhaps you wish to remember those you have cared for, or currently care for, and to honour the love you both give and receive. Maybe you need to take time to appreciate who you are and the unique gifts you have been given to share with others on this life's journey. You may simply decide to have a moment in which to nourish your own spirit, in order that you may return to the world whole, and healed and able to lighten the burden of others who struggle with the demands of this life. Settle for a while now in this sacred place, and allow yourself to connect with the energies of the Mother.

***

Now, as you sit in this peaceful place, you gradually become aware that the beautiful voices have quietened, and as you look around, you see that the candle flame has also grown dim. You slowly rise to your feet and stand before the altar, giving thanks to the Mother for holding this sacred space just for you, here, within the womb of the Earth.

Slowly, slowly now, you turn and begin to walk back through the chamber into the softly lit entrance. Here you stand for a moment at the mouth of the cave, savouring this rebirth as you once again step out onto the beach, beneath the full light of the Mother Moon, and begin to retrace your steps along the sand.

Now, whenever the time feels right, gradually bring yourself back to the awareness of the present, and when you feel ready, you may open your eyes.

Full Moon Superstitions and Folklore

The Full Moon is thought to be an auspicious time for:

- Slaughtering animals for food as the meat will be sweeter.
- Being born, as the child will have a long, prosperous and healthy life.
- Buying and selling goods.

The Full Moon is thought to be inauspicious for:

- Medical treatment
- Falling ill, as it denotes a lengthy illness
- Making major decisions
- Cutting hair as it grows too fast
- Beginning journeys
- Moving house
- Starting a business
- Cutting out a dress

In Ireland, it is said that if you walk nine times round a *faery rath* (fairy hill) at the full Moon, you will be able to find the entrance.

In Wales, fishermen avoid looking at what they call the 'Moon line', which is the reflection of the full Moon making a line of light across the water when setting out to sea, as this is seen as a bad omen, whilst in other areas, fishermen say that you should make a wish when crossing the Moon line.

One of the best-known folk tales connected with the full Moon is that of the *Lycanthrope* or Werewolf. In the Nordic and Saxon traditions, mythical creatures such as dragons and werewolves, were accepted as being real creatures, all of which were respected, revered, and feared, in equal measure. These Teutonic people also held a strong belief in the fact that all men had the capability of changing themselves at will, into animals of all kinds, one of which was the wolf.

The reason a man might become a wolf was twofold. The first, was that he might consciously decide to do so, in order to attack his enemies, or feed upon their flocks, something that was far easier to accomplish as a werewolf than a mere man. The second, was that this metamorphosis was involuntary, and most likely due to some sort of sorcery, practiced by an adept occultist at the time of the full Moon. Here the unfortunate victim would be forced to change into a werewolf, therefore becoming quite oblivious to the carnage he caused, and powerless to stop it.

A Norse tale tells of two men, Sigmund and Sinfjoth, who were wandering through a forest one night, when they came upon a cabin in which two men were sleeping. They noticed immediately that hanging above the sleeping men, on a hook in the wall, were two wolf skins.

Unbeknown to Sigmund and Sinfjoth, the two sleeping men were actually werewolves who had been bewitched. As an act of compassion however, the sorcerer allowed the two men a period of twenty-four hours every ten days, in which they were free to discard their wolf skins and resume their human form, and it was during this time that Sigmund and Sinfjoth came upon them.

Sigmund and Sinfjoth decided that they would try the wolf skins on, but as soon as they did so the skins held firm, and they were unable to get them off. Much to their horror they too became victims of the sorcerer's enchantment, and were immediately transformed into werewolves. All at once they began to howl, and bite both the sleeping men, and each other.

After ten days of death and destruction, the wolf skins fell away from them and they returned to their human form. Fortunately for Sigmund and Sinfjoth, they had retained the horrific memories of what they had done, and so immediately burned the skins, at which point the spell of the sorcerer was broken, and the werewolves were no more.

Full Moon Celebrations and Rituals

A Moon celebration, regardless of the phase, can be as simple, or as complex as you wish, depending on preference and/or experience.

If you are well versed in formal magickal practice and wish to cast a spell, then the casting of a circle, changing your consciousness, path working, and both feeling and visualising the outcome, will most probably form part of your Moon ritual.

However, if you just wish to acknowledge a particular Moon phase, then simply light a candle, burn incense or oils, play music of your choice and perhaps use some of the suggestions given below to formulate your own Moon celebration.

A Full Moon Altar

You may wish to set up a small altar in your home or garden, and incorporate any of the following as decoration, or use ideas of your own.

- A dish, bowl or chalice of water to represent the pull of the tides.
- White, silver or gold candles to mirror the colours of the Moon.
- A white, silver or gold altar cloth.
- White, gold, or red flowers to represent the full orb, or the Mother aspect of the Moon (red can symbolise menstrual blood or the blood of life).
- A crystal ball to represent the full orb.
- Eggs, to represent the golden orb, and also its elliptical orbit.

- A Moonstone, pearls or silver, all of which are sacred to the Moon.
- A statue to represent the Mother Goddess (Diana, Demeter, Selene, Luna).
- Something that symbolises what you are attempting to bring to fruition, or honour. If you planted seeds at the new Moon, and they are now flourishing, place these on your altar.

Honouring the full Moon usually takes place either the day before, the day following, or the day of its full phase. If the Moon is visible in the sky, this will always add a little magick to your workings, especially if you can go outside to either stand, or work, beneath Her.

If however, the weather is inclement and you must remain indoors, remember that the Moon is still there so simply light a candle, or place a crystal ball on the altar, as a symbolic reminder.

In order to prepare yourself, you may wish to take a few moments in which to mediate on what the full Moon means to you, and the action you need to take in order that your new Moon desires are being brought to fruition. Alternatively, you may wish to use the guided visualization above.

Full Moon Magick

The full Moon is all about bringing things to fruition, before reaping the benefits, albeit it in some cases, it may take a further full lunar cycle before results are seen, dependent upon the type of magick woven. What follows is a generic full Moon blessing spell, to bless those desires which you visualised, and gave energy to at the new Moon.

An Incense Blessing Spell

You will need:

- A feather
- Something that symbolises your goal
- A small jar
- A bowl
- A teaspoon
- Mortar and pestle (two teaspoons can be used as a substitute)
- A charcoal block
- An incense, or fire-proof burner (Do not use an oil burner as the heat from the charcoal will crack it)
- Full Moon blessing incense (see recipe below)

Full Moon Blessing Incense Ingredients:

N.B. If you don't have all the ingredients, then just adapt the recipe accordingly.

Your intent, plus the herbs and resins you do have will work just as well.

- 1 teaspoon Myrrh resin, crushed to gravel size
- 1 teaspoon Sandarac resin, crushed to gravel size
- 1 teaspoon Frankincense resin, crushed to gravel size
- 5 Juniper berries
- 1 teaspoon Rose petals
- 1/2 teaspoon Lavender flowers
- 1/2 teaspoon Mugwort
- 1/2 teaspoon dried Fennel seeds or leaves

- 1 teaspoon Chamomile flowers
- 6 drops Sandalwood oil

Method:

Mix each of the ingredients one by one in a bowl, stirring as you do so, and focussing your intent on the outcome you desire.

When the incense is made, transfer it to a tightly sealed jar, making sure you label and date it. Use within three months to ensure that it remains charged and fresh.

Casting your spell:

Light a charcoal block, and place it in a fireproof container or incense burner.

Take the item that symbolises you goal, and place it on your altar, or close to your incense burner.

When the charcoal block has just turned grey, sprinkle on a little of the incense, and as it begins to smoke, take your feather and begin wafting the blessing smoke over the object that symbolises your goal, whilst saying the following blessing, adapting the full Moon blessing below, or writing your own:

> *The full Moon's beauty fills the skies*
> *Now may my goals be blessed and rise*
> *On sacred smoke, brushed feather light,*
> *To reach Diana, Queen of Night.*

Leave the charcoal block to cool completely before you dispose of it.

Full Moon Blessing

Lady of fecundity,
Bless my labours
As they ripen
Beneath your gaze,
Leading me to experience
Your abundant generosity.

Toasting the Full Moon

You may wish to raise a toast to the full Moon, to simply acknowledge Her presence, or to give thanks.

Appropriate drinks include rose wine, red wine, or a red juice such as cranberry or cherry, as they symbolise the birth blood or menstrual blood of the Mother, as we honour Her at her full phase. Alternatively try white or golden drinks to symbolise the full orb, such as white wine, elderflower cordial, apple juice or honeyed mead.

You may also wish to partake of some food in order to ground yourself, especially if you have carried out a meditation, or other form of spell work. Moon cakes or other small round cakes, buns and breads are ideal, or if you prefer a healthier option, then yellow or white rounded fruits, such as lychees or grapefruit will suffice.

The full Mother Moon represents the beautiful and creative facets of all women, whether this is though childbirth, or other innovative projects. The Mother, like the Maiden and the Enchantress, will always live within us regardless of our age, for each of us has the ability to care, to nurture, and to create. So, when the full golden orb next visits our skies, honour Her presence and begin to realise your full potential as you blossom, and bloom into the person you were born to be.

Mrs Darley Tale: The Mistress of Illusion

Twilight was just closing in as we left the pub in the village at the top of the lane, and the late June evening was unusually warm for our corner of Bodmin Moor. Sharp Tor stood dark and proud against the streaky remnants of a cobalt sky, whilst the unmistakable aroma of moorland ferns and sedge grass filled the air, as our merry band of five ventured off down the lane.

'First one to spot a glow worm gets to open Bod's bottle of pre-birthday malt,' said Rose.

'And what if I win?' asked Lucy.

'You will get a glass of my delicious elderflower cordial my dear,' said Mrs Darley.

Bod turned towards Rose, 'I notice how you're quick to offer *my* whiskey as a prize and not your own sloe gin.'

'Well, I'm glad Rose offered your whiskey as the prize, Bod,' said Mrs Darley, laughing, 'because I've just spotted a glow worm, over there in the crevice of that drystone wall, and I'm none too partial to gin.'

We all gathered round to see the fascinating fluorescent emerald light that emanated from the larva of a female beetle, acting as a beacon to prospective mates.

I remember being entranced by seeing my very first glow-worm the previous year, when I had taken a short cut across the moor on my way home from a barn dance and now, seeing one for the second time, did nothing to diminish my sense of wonder.

'They are so beautiful,' I murmured, crouching down beside the wall to get a better look.

Mrs Darley smiled. 'They are indeed, my dear. A real bit of midsummer magick.'

'Oh, look out, here comes Phyllis,' said Rose, as a small white car headed towards us down the lane. 'She'll be wondering why we haven't got very far.'

When we had suggested a midsummer sojourn to the pub at the top of the lane earlier on that evening, Phyllis had said that she couldn't walk the mile both there and back, and so intended to drive, whilst giving us walkers a head start each way.

Upon Rose's suggestion, we all joined hands and stood across the road to form a roadblock, laughing as we flagged Phyllis down.

'Goodness me,' said Phyllis peering out of the car window and saying exactly what Rose had predicted, 'you haven't got very far.'

'We were glow worm spotting, dear,' said Mrs Darley, 'hence our delay.'

'And now we're going back to Mrs D's to open Bod's early birthday present of a bottle of Irish malt,' said Rose.

'Well in that case, I'll see you down there,' said Phyllis, waving as she drove off down the lane. 'Don't be too long.'

With no more glow worms to delay us, and the promise of Irish malt to spur us on, we soon arrived at the cottages. Bod called in at his home on the lane to pick up his whiskey, whilst the rest of us continued round to Mrs Darley's cottage, where Phyllis had already lit the candles, and placed the best whiskey glasses out on the table.

'Oh, well done, dear,' said Mrs Darley. 'I think you'll find there are some cheese twists in the kitchen cupboard if you would be so kind.'

Soon Bod arrived, at which point the whiskey was opened, and our glasses filled.

Mrs Darley turned to Bod and raised her glass. 'To you, my dear, early though it may be, and as your second half century dawns, may the gods bring you blessings of love, health, and wisdom, on this, your fiftieth birthday.'

'Hear, hear,' we chorused.

'And the occasional good Irish Malt,' laughed Rose.

'Oh my goodness,' said Phyllis, suddenly pointing towards the window. 'Just look at that Moon.'

We all murmured in wonder as we turned to watch the most enormous golden orb rise above the far horizon of Dartmoor.

'Well, it is supposed to be one of the closest Moons of the year to earth,' said Mrs Darley.

'But it looks so big, as though you could almost touch it,' said Rose, 'and look at the colour, it's almost like ... well like...'

'Rich ochre?' suggested Phyllis.

'Well yes... yes... I suppose it is.'

'I don't think I've ever seen anything quite like it,' I said.

Bod nodded. 'Yes, it's certainly impressive, but it will soon return to its original size as it rises in the sky.'

I was intrigued. 'But what makes it so large when it's rising?'

'It's all an optical illusion, isn't it dear?' said Mrs Darley, turning to Phyllis.

Phyllis nodded. 'It is indeed. It's the atmospheric conditions that make the difference. Back in Aristotle's time, the Earth's atmosphere was certainly thought to magnify the Moon as it came over the horizon. Today however, the consensus of opinion is that both a rising Moon, and a Moon that is high in the sky, are exactly the same size.'

'But they can't be,' said Rose. 'I mean, look at that.' She pointed towards the window, outside of which the Moon seemed to hover like a great balloon.

'Here's how you can prove it for yourself,' said Phyllis. 'Tomorrow night, just as the Moon becomes visible above the horizon, roll up a piece of paper into a tube, making the circumference so as it just fits the Moon and secure it with a piece of tape. Then, look through the same tube again when the Moon is overhead, and you will find that the rising Moon, and high Moon, are exactly the same size.'

Lucy tugged at Rose's arm. 'Can we do that, Mum?'

'Of course,' said Rose, smiling. 'But I still don't really understand *why* the Moon looks so big when it appears just above the horizon.'

'When the Moon rises,' said Phyllis, 'we measure its size against objects here on earth, such as buildings and trees, mountains and tors, and our brains inflate its size, so that the Moon appears to be a huge body compared with them. When the Moon rises higher in the sky however, all we have to measure it against is the vast infinity of space, hence it looks small in comparison.'

'Mmm,' I said, 'that makes sense.'

'It's called the Ponzo Illusion,' said Phyllis, 'named after the Italian psychologist Mario Ponzo, in 1911.'

Rose frowned, still puzzled. 'How do you know all this, Phyllis?'

'She wasn't a headmistress all those years for nothing,' said Mrs Darley.

'But I thought you taught history,' said Rose.

'Amongst other things,' smiled Phyllis, 'but science was also a passion.'

'That's interesting,' said Bod, 'and has reminded me of a something my father showed me as a kid. Has anyone got any small change?'

We all began to feel in pockets and look in purses, tipping our offerings onto the table, and watched as Bod arranged six fifty-pence pieces in a circle, and six five-pence pieces in another circle. He then placed a two-pence piece in the centre of each circle, and, turning to Lucy said, 'so which centre piece is bigger?'

There was a moment's silence, whilst Lucy wrestled with

her answer.

'I want to say that one,' she said, pointing to the circle surrounded by five pence pieces, 'but I know the coins in the middle are both 2p's.'

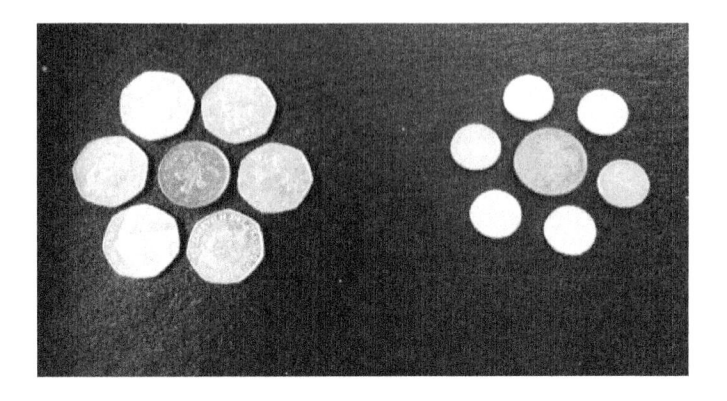

An example of the Ebbinghaus Illusion

'Exactly, Lucy,' smiled Phyllis. 'What your dad has just shown us is called the Ebbinghaus Illusion, and it proves absolutely what we were saying about the Moon.'

'How?'

'Well, the two-pence pieces represent the Moon, whilst the other coins represent its backdrop. So the two-pence in the centre of the five-pence pieces, is like the Moon rising against comparatively small objects of buildings and mountains here on earth. This is what makes the two-pence, or the Moon, look huge. Meanwhile, the two-pence sitting in the centre of the fifty-pence pieces, is like the Moon rising against the vastness of space, which makes the Moon look small in comparison.'

'That's brilliant,' said Lucy, 'I'm going to show everyone at school on Monday.'

'Look,' said Rose, pointing out of the window, 'already the Moon looks so much smaller, now it's risen higher into the sky.'

'Well my dears,' said Mrs Darley, 'the Moon isn't called 'the Mistress of Illusion' for nothing.'

'What do you mean?' I asked.

'The presence of the Moon my dear, changes everything. Beneath Her light, faces and landscapes look more beautiful, lovers feel more amorous, smugglers heed the call to adventure, and as for us magickal folk...' She let the sentence drift away.

Part of me wanted to ask what she meant by 'us magickal folk', yet another part of me was afraid to hear the answer.

I looked questioningly at her, hoping she might explain, but she merely smiled as though hugging a secret, and just for a moment, I felt like an outsider in a world I didn't really understand.

The following poem was written in empathy for those who might simultaneously love, and yet are also horrified, by the uncontrollable urges of their werewolf lover, especially during the full light of the Moon, when he is unable to resist the call of his other mistress.

Change

I stretch out my hand across the bed.
The sheets are cold,
Your absence old.

Unable to soothe my heart - it aches,
Like an old scar.
I know where you are.

The room silvers as gathered-clouds part.
I know why you cheat.
I cannot compete.

My mirrored image cries salted tears,
From eyes made bright
By full Moon's light.

If I had courage, I would take your life,
Sever the thread,
Prevent the dread

That accompanies each moonlit night
You go to her,
With lycanthrope fur.

Chapter Ten

Waning Moon Magick

Gradually, the brightness of the full Moon gives way to a gentler light, as little by little She diminishes and the night skies grow darker. Once again during the waning phase, there is equilibrium between the dark and light halves of the Moon, and although the second quarter still signifies a time of harmony and balance, this is a quieter period, when the benefits of any labours can begin to be enjoyed.

This is a time of satisfaction, a time of consolidation and settling. This is when we can begin to enjoy the relationship we have embarked upon, to feel more settled in our new job, or to see where our life path is leading us.

Waning Moon magick teaches us to honour not only our outer persona, but also our hidden shadow, for it is a combination of both that makes us who we are. This Moon phase is associated with the magick of transformation, wisdom, and if necessary, carefully considered banishing.

This is the time when the face of the Mother turns towards that of the Wise Woman (or Sage for men) and our Goddess, for the waning Moon is Hecate, Greek Goddess of Witchcraft, Magick, and the Night.

Hecate, whose name can be translated as 'far fleeting', or 'the distant one', was once a triple Goddess of Earth, Sky, and Sea. Her domain extended into both the heavens and the underworld, for it was from Her, all things came, and it was to Her, that all things were destined to return.

Legend tells us that she was later incorporated into Titan culture, where She became the daughter of the Star

Goddess Asteria and Persaios, son of Eurybia. It was said that Asteria abandoned Hecate at the crossroads, where She was taken in and brought up by shepherds, hence Her association with the crossroads, and being the protector of flocks. This act of human kindness by the shepherds was never forgotten by Hecate, and as such, She cultivated an empathy with human suffering, making Her a much-loved Goddess, both in ancient and present times.

Hecate also became an important figure in Greek mythology, where She was often said to be the daughter of Zeus and Hera. She was worshipped in many Athenian households, and revered as Goddess of Protection, and Prosperity. Although She initially retained Her reputation as a triple Goddess of Earth, Sky, and Sea, She was also revered as a dual Goddess, one who brought death, yet who was also invoked as a midwife at the birth of a child. It was this association with fertility that led many of Her worshippers to carry the torches of Hecate around the fields before planting, to ensure that the forthcoming season would be abundant.

Latterly however, Her darker aspect superceded all others, and She primarily took on the role of the Wise Woman or Crone, through which She became known as the Goddess of many things including witchcraft, magick, necromancy, sorcery, poisonous herbs, and the Moon. She was usually portrayed holding a pair of torches, keys or daggers, whilst dogs and serpents were Her totem animals. This more sombre role can be traced through a story involving Hecate, Her mother Hera, Her father Zeus, and Zeus' lover Europa.

One day, after watching Her mother applying her makeup, Hecate stole some of Hera's rouge to give to Europa, Her father's mistress. Upon discovering what Hecate had done, Hera was furious, and in order to escape

Her Mother's wrath, Hecate flew to Earth, where She hid in the house of woman who was in labour.

After helping the woman give birth, Hecate was then deemed unclean, due to the fact that the birthing process was associated with infection and death. Hecate was not therefore permitted to re-enter the court of Zeus.

Knowing however, that Hera would continue to track Her down, Hecate next took refuge in a funeral procession, which cemented Her association with the dead and dying.

Throughout Her escapades, Hecate's actions were constantly being monitored by the underworld deities, who eventually transported Her to the flooding underworld waters of the river Acheron. Here it would have been easy for Hecate to allow the raging river to destroy Her, but instead, not only did She decide to embrace her new environment, but She also took on the role of the dark Mother and the Wise Woman and as such, became well versed in the crafting of darker magicks.

We all have a shadow side, a side that many of us would prefer to deny. This part of us however, should not only be acknowledged, but also celebrated, and as the Moon begins to wane, Hecate teaches us that moving away from the bright light of the full Moon into darker times, is a necessary requirement for living a balanced life.

Hecate's act of stealing Her Mother's rouge triggered a string of events, through which Hecate gains wisdom, and also learns to accept responsibility for Her own actions. She does not condone Her Father and His mistress's behaviour but, rather than take sides, She accepts Europa for who she is and is willing to risk the subsequent wrath of Her Mother.

She also learns that Her actions have consequences, and chooses to flee to the mortal realm rather than face Her Mother's anger. She not only enters the home of a pregnant woman, but risks everything to become Her midwife, an act She knows will prevent Her ever returning to the court of Her father, Zeus.

Hecate is then taken into the Underworld, a situation She again accepts is of Her own making, and as such embraces Her new role, as the Dark Mother and Wise Woman. This illustrates that change is part and parcel of life, and that life and death are simply different sides of the same coin.

This story of Hecate shows that as the age of the Mother slides into that of the Wise Woman, it should be a time to be embraced, for it heralds a period of liberation from both menstruation and family duties. It not only offers us the opportunity to return to the longed-for freedom of Maiden and Enchantress days, but now we also have the added benefit of wisdom, and experience, which together make a heady and powerful cocktail of attraction.

Sadly however, the age of the Wise Woman is often dreaded in our culture, and is seen as the time when a woman's useful life is coming to an end. Her reproductive life is over and – in the eyes of society at least – her looks are diminishing and she is becoming less desirable sexually. At best, she is led to believe that she might just be able to sustain a career, or become a grandmother, and at worst, she can expect the immediate onset of arthritis and the added adornment of a hairy wart.

It is this latter, negative image that many women dread. Added to this, comes the often, stressful experience of the menopause and the uncomfortable symptoms this can bring, whilst also attempting to fit in with society's prescribed idea of what the life of an older woman should be like.

Perhaps therefore, it is time we released consensus truth, stood out from the crowd, cast our inhibitions to the winds and opened our arms in order to embrace the new life that is about to unfold.

Waning Moon, Wise Woman Meditation:

Sit quietly, somewhere you will not be disturbed. Play music, burn incense or oils of your choice (Those which have cleansing and releasing properties, such as Juniper, Cypress, Rosemary or Marjoram, are all appropriate for meditations beneath the waning Moon) and begin to become aware of your breathing, don't try to alter it in any way, but just become aware of its gentle rhythm, as you breathe in and out... in and out.

Now imagine you are walking through the woods on a bright autumn evening. The last rays of the Sun are pleasantly warm, and the trees are richly dressed in scarlet and gold, forming a foliate archway through which to pass. You glance down at the path as it winds its way deeper into the woods, and become fascinated by the beautiful array of fungi, which seemingly spring up beneath your feet. The brambles reach out to you, and you stop to taste the juicy blackberries that adorn each branch.

As you continue to walk along the path, you suddenly become aware that the Sun is beginning to sink, the light is fading and a cool wind is rippling through the trees, dislodging the leaves which spiral like confetti towards the forest floor and suddenly your way is lost. You shiver and pull your cloak tightly around you as you wonder which way to turn, for now grey clouds gather, and dusk begins to fall.

It is therefore with much relief that you notice a small wooden cabin just ahead of you, from which shines a welcoming light. As you draw closer, you see that the door is slightly ajar, and you decide to enter.

Once inside, you are almost overwhelmed with a wonderful array of sights and delicious smells. For you see that you are standing in a store cupboard, where every shelf is covered with exotic urns of aromatic spices, jars of juicy jams and baskets of plump autumn fruits.

You are mesmerised by this treasure of nature's bounty, and as you wander around the shelves, you begin to touch, smell and taste all the wonderful foods that are on display. You instantly appreciate how each fruit and spice began life as a young seed, that had to be nurtured and tended in order to form the basic ingredients from which the most magickal produce has evolved.

You realise that this is the natural way of things, and that nature is illustrating to you the journey from Maiden to Enchantress, from Enchantress to Mother, and from Mother to Wise Woman, with the latter, perhaps, being the richest age of all.

This store cupboard reminds you to be appreciative of the wisdom you hold and for the ability to share that wisdom with others. It illustrates all the good things that are present in your life, and you realise that these things can only be appreciated by having lived a life that has known both the light, and the shadow.

Spend some time now in this wonderful place, feasting upon the beauty that surrounds you, and when the time feels right, choose something from the shelves that particularly appeals to you. It may be the rich exotic spices, that will symbolically call you to do something exciting and different with your life. It may be a jar of jam, that will remind you to let a little sweetness into your daily routine, or it may be a juicy plump fruit with which you can quench your thirst when life becomes dry and parched of goodness. This is your personal harvest upon which you can now feed, bringing nourishment to body and soul.

***

It is now almost time to leave your store cupboard, but be assured that you can visit this wonderful place any time you wish, to avail yourself of its treasures. So, whenever you are ready, begin to make your way out through the door of the cabin, taking a moment to glance up at the sky through the canopy of trees. You see that the darkness is now beginning to fade as the dawn breaks in the east, and the waning crescent Moon hangs high in the ever-lightening sky.

You smile and nod at Her, suddenly filled with gratitude and appreciation for being allowed to enter and experience this rich phase of your life. Then, with ease of the Mother, the self-assurance of the Enchantress, the light footedness of the Maiden, and the wisdom of the Wise Woman, you begin retracing your steps back through the woods to where your journey began.

Now, whenever the time feels right, slowly bring yourself back to the awareness of the present, and when you feel ready, you may open your eyes.

Waning Moon Superstitions and Folklore

The Waning Moon is considered an auspicious time for:

- Correcting mistakes
- Settling disputes
- Taking things apart and tearing things down
- Getting rid of bad habits and addictions
- Getting divorced
- Changing restrictive thought patterns

- A hair cut (especially if you don't want your hair to re-grow quickly)
- Stuffing your feather bed (if you possess one)
- Washing your linen as the dirt will disappear with the diminishing light

Likewise, it is considered an inauspicious time for:

- Buying or wearing a new dress
- Marriage

Waning Moon Celebrations and Rituals

A Moon celebration, regardless of the phase, can be as simple or as complex as you wish, depending on preference and/or experience.

If you are well-versed in formal magickal practice and wish to cast a spell, then the casting of a circle, changing your consciousness, path working, and both feeling and visualising the outcome, will most probably form part of your Moon ritual.

If however, you just wish to acknowledge a particular Moon phase, then simply light a candle, burn incense or oils, play music of your choice, and perhaps use some of the suggestions given below to formulate your own Moon celebration.

A Waning Moon Altar

You may wish to set up a small altar in your home or garden, and incorporate one of the following as decoration, or alternatively use ideas of your own.

- A dish, bowl or chalice of water to represent the pull of the tides.
- Black and white (or silver) candles to represent the light and dark half of the Moon.
- A purple or dark cloth on your altar.
- Contrasting colours of flowers to represent both halves of the Moon – purple and yellow, deep blue and orange, or red and white.
- A Yin and Yang sign to represent the two halves of the Moon.
- A statue to represent a Dark Goddess or Crone (Hecate, Ceridwen).
- Something to represent what you are harvesting in your life, or to celebrate what has come to fruition. It may be something you have actually produced, or a bowl of fruit, which generally symbolises the ripening of a project. Scissors are also appropriate to represent a habit or something that is being taken out of your life. If your planted seeds are in flower, or fruiting, you may wish to pick, or cut your crop.

Honouring the waning Moon can take place any time from two days after the full Moon, to two days before dark Moon, according to the changes you wish to manifest in your life. If possible, go outside and stand beneath Her, even if it is only briefly, albeit She rises late into the evening or early morning.

The waning Moon, just like the waxing Moon, offers you the opportunity to bring balance into your life as the second quarter phase comes into being a week after the full Moon is past. Here, you may like to light black and white candles to represent the light and dark halves of the Moon, or to hold a yin and yang symbol, symbolising harmony and balance.

Perhaps there is something you wish to take out of your life, such as a habit or practice that no longer serves you. If this is the case, you may wish to cut the ties that bind, by symbolically cutting them with scissors or a knife. Please note however, that If you usually use an athame during your magickal work, this is not the tool with which to perform this act. Use your boline, a working knife, or scissors instead.

The waning Moon is a time to enjoy the fruits of your labour and give thanks for what has come into your life during this lunar cycle. Many people feel that whatever you appreciate and give thanks for, will return to you in abundance. This may also be an opportune time to make a donation to a chosen charity, or to help someone by giving of your time.

When the waning Moon next visits our skies, honour what the Wise Woman means to you as She evaporates into the darkness. You may wish to take a few moments in which to meditate, or perhaps use the guided visualisation above.

Waning Moon Magick

The waning Moon is either about giving thanks and reaping the benefits of that which you have sown, or cutting the emotional ties that bind you to a habit or person that no longer form part of your life.

What follows are two generic Moon spells, which can be moulded and shaped to suit various needs.

Cutting the ties spell

You will need:

- A raw egg
- A marker pen
- Lavender oil or Lavender tea

Casting your spell:

Take time to be still and to engage the power of your mind, emotions and senses, to focus on that which you no longer wish to be a part of your life. Concentrate on how it feels to have this in your life. Do you feel controlled, anger, hatred, guilt, shame, frustration or fear?

Now take your egg, and still retaining all those emotions, begin to inscribe them onto the shell with your marker pen. Say each word aloud as you write it.

'I transfer this anger/guilt/ etc., to this egg.'

Wrap the egg up safely, and if you can, either go to a crossroads (sacred to Hecate), or simply draw a cross in the soil in your garden where you wish to perform the spell.

Now take out the egg, bring all those negative emotions to mind for one last time and then smash the egg down onto the ground, or into the Earth, taking care not to let any splash on you.

Turn away, and don't look back. Think only positive thoughts as you walk or drive back home. Picture your life now that these negative emotions are gone. How do you feel - happy, relieved, strong, courageous, peaceful or free?

When you return home, burn some Lavender oil in an oil

burner or diffuser, have a Lavender bath, or drink some Lavender tea. This will help cleanse both yourself and the room of any remaining negative energies and bring about a peaceful atmosphere in which to begin this new phase of your life.

(Please note: Do not use Lavender oil in a bath, or drink Lavender tea if you are either in the first trimester of pregnancy or if you have low blood pressure. You can, however, burn a couple of drops safely on an oil burner).

An Appreciation Tree Spell

You will need:

- Either a live pot plant, which can take the weight of pieces of card or paper being hung upon it, or a few twigs from the woods.
- If you are using twigs, you will need a plant pot containing Earth, or a mound of plasticine in which to place or secure your twigs.
- Several small pieces of card or paper (5 x 2cm approximately) with a hole punched in each.
- Cotton, ribbon or string.

Casting your spell:

- Take a moment once your tree is ready and in place, to bless and dedicate it to the purpose for which it is intended. Use the following, or perhaps write your own:

To my appreciation tree
My blessings now I give to thee,
May all that I acknowledge here
Increase and grow throughout the year.

- Take time to be still and to engage the power of your mind, emotions, and senses, to focus on anything in your life for which you are truly grateful. Think of how these things or people make you feel – loved, safe, satisfied, proud, happy, protected or joyful.
- Now take a piece of card or paper, thread it with ribbon or string, and retaining all those positive emotions, write a sentence that describes the first thing that you are grateful for.
- Now say out loud, 'I appreciate/am grateful for whoever or whatever is on your piece of paper, and hang it on your tree.
- Repeat steps 3 and 4 as many times as are necessary.

You can keep the tree on your altar, or in a special place in your home, where you can be reminded, especially on days which are not so bright, of the good things in your life. The tree can be added to at any time, or you may wish to revisit it only at the waning Moon and make this a regular ritual. Occasionally the pieces of card may need to be replaced or changed as your life continually moves forward. If you are using a live plant, remember to water and nourish it, so that your blessings grow.

Waning Moon Blessing

Lady of wisdom,
As darkness descends,
Let me come to know my shadow,
In order that my life
May be lived in harmony.

Toasting the Waning Moon

You may wish to raise a toast to the waning Moon, to simply acknowledge Her presence, or to give thanks. Red wine, port, black currant juice, or elderberry cordial, are all appropriate drinks with which to honour the diminishing light of the waning Moon.

You may also wish to partake of some food in order to ground yourself, especially if you have carried out a meditation, or other form of spell work. A marbled cake, or white and brown bread, make suitable waning Moon food, as they represent the dark and light sides of the Moon.

The Wise Woman's Moon represents the wisdom and beauty that is to be found in age. Impetuosity is replaced by calm understanding, and searching is replaced by a deep well of knowing. Yet Maiden, Enchantress, and Mother also lie within the Wise Woman's psyche, making her both complete and balanced.

Mrs Darley Tale: The Gift

Rose stood on my doorstep one Saturday morning in July, holding an envelope in her outstretched hand.

'An invitation for you', she said smiling. 'It's for Bod's unmentionable birthday party. It's a surprise, and I'm not sure how he'll take it, but I've invited lots of people he used to know, I think there's about fifty or so - one for every year,' she laughed. 'It'll be at The Magpie, just down off the moor there, do you know it?'

I nodded. 'I've never been in though.'

'It's nice inside, old and quaint, and we can have half of it to ourselves. I've organised it for next Friday night, as that's the closest weekend to his birthday. Can you come?'

'I wouldn't miss it for the world,' I said. 'Thank you.'

'See you there about eight-ish then.'

With a quick wave of her hand she was gone, and I spent the rest of the day deliberating what to buy Bod for his birthday.

***

The following Friday evening was beautiful, still, and surprisingly quite warm at half past seven, when I went around to collect Mrs Darley and Phyllis from next door.

The Magpie was overflowing with both cars and people when we arrived, so I dropped Mrs Darley and Phyllis off outside, whilst I drove off to abandon my car further up the lane.

Returning to the pub, I fought my way in through the crowds and noticed Mrs Darley signalling to me with a wave of her hand. As I approached the cosy looking corner table which was wedged into the alcove alongside the open log fire, I saw that she was holding court, surrounded by Phyllis, Peter, Eddie, Don, and two elderly gentlemen, one of whom seemed vaguely familiar, although the other I didn't recognise.

The former gentleman was small and rather weather-beaten, sporting what looked like a 1920's suit, complete with watch and chain and wearing a well-worn black cap upon his head. The latter was an extremely elegant Chinese gentleman with a long thin beard, silver glasses, and dressed in a pale green mandarin tunic over light cotton trousers.

As I arrived at the table, both gentlemen stood and allowed me to squeeze into a corner of the alcove seat, and whilst Eddie went to the bar to get me a drink, the introductions were made.

The man in the suit was introduced rather mysteriously as 'Black Bill', who I recognised as the man who had been asked over to Mrs Darley's on the morning of the Spring Equinox, to judge the egg decorating competition.

'Coalman dear', whispered Mrs Darley.

'Oh,' I said, feeling somewhat disappointed in what seemed a rather mundane explanation for such an enigmatic name.

The Chinese gentleman meanwhile, rose from his seat and bowed courteously, introducing himself as 'Chan Yin'. I waited, expecting Mrs Darley to explain a little more about him, but with no explanation forthcoming, I settled into our tight-knit corner for what was to be an entertaining evening of anecdotes, by and about Bod, together with mysterious tales of the moor.

As the evening progressed, the rather romantic subject of Cornish smugglers came to the fore, at which point Black Bill leaned forward in a rather conspiratorial way and announced that his great-great-grandfather had been involved in the business of 'free-trading', as he preferred to call it.

'It's still smuggling, Bill, whatever terminology you care to use,' laughed Don.

'But the taxes back then - they were cripplin',' protested Black Bill.

'Not much changed there then,' laughed Eddie the poacher, who was not averse to carrying out a little smuggling himself.

'Ah, but back in 1815,' said Black Bill, 'there were around fourteen hundred items subject to import duty, and these were everyday things like tea, stockings, 'ats, spices, sugar, playing cards, and 'andkerchiefs, apart from the usual alcohol and tobacco.

'Make no doubt, the duty was sky 'igh, and that's why free traders risked their lives to bring goods into the country. In fact, nearly everybody 'ad their 'ands on smuggled goods at some point, whether they realised it or not. Even shop goods might've been smuggled in, you just never knew. It's not like today when people smuggle illegal things in, like narcotics and arms.'

'So, how was your great-great-grandfather involved?' I asked.

'Ah yes, Thomas Pengelly,' said Black Bill wistfully, ''Ee was quite an infamous free-trader who helped bring goods in, and take 'em out.'

'Out?' I asked, 'I thought smugglers only brought goods in?'

'Strictly speaking that's true, my 'ansome,' said Black Bill with a smile. 'The term 'smuggler' was used to describe them who imported, while them who managed to get goods out of the country without paying export duty, were known as 'owlers'.'

'Why 'owlers', Bill?' Asked Phyllis.

'Don't know, mebbe 'cuz they worked at night, like the owl, but then the same could be said for smugglers. Anyways, export duty 'ad to be paid on goods leaving the country, and like import duty, it was cripplin'.'

'I had no idea about that,' I said.

'Back in the thirteenth century see,' Black Bill continued, ''eavy duties was payable on every sack of wool going out of the country, but back in old Thomas' time it was tin and copper, that was the main export. I 'ave 'eard tell that as much as seventy five percent of total tin and copper production was illegally shipped abroad.

'Course, other products also went over the water to France, like needles and woollen goods, which could be sold over there for an 'efty profit. I've even 'eard tell that during the Napoleonic wars, gold was smuggled over to France, so as Napoleon could pay his armies. Mind you,' he said, 'that wasn't done from down 'ere, that was the Sussex and Kent boys.'

'So what did your great-great-grandfather actually do?' I tried my question again.

'Ah yes, well Thomas Pengelly, 'ee was one of the transporters. See, the smuggling operation needed four or five key-folk, or groups of folk.'

'The first was called a 'venturer'. Now 'ee put up the money and was often a landowner, or even a magistrate, and 'ee would commission the captain of a smuggling vessel and 'is crew to go and pick up certain goods from across the channel, usually France, sometimes the Channel Islands.'

'When they returned with the goods, they would rely on someone on dry land to let 'em know if the coast was clear, such as lightin' a fire on the 'eadland or, as the famous smuggler Jack Corlyon of Coverack used to do - give 'is wife 'is red shirt to wash when 'ee went away, and if it was on the line when 'ee returned, 'ee knew it was safe to land. Mind you they normally waited 'til dark, and always tried to pick the dark nights of the Moon.'

'A night like this would be no good then Bill?' said Phyllis, gesturing to the full Moon that was now visible through the un-curtained window.

Black Bill shook his head. 'No, a night like this, when the full Silver Lady 'angs in the sky. That 'ud be no good for smuggling. The Moon was never the smugglers friend, see?'

We all nodded our understanding, not wanting to interrupt Bill's story.

'Then there were the 'batmen', he continued. 'They wuz a necessary evil, protecting the smugglers as they wuz unloading the cargo, and roping it up the cliffs to safety. See, if the customs men came, then the batmen would… well… fight 'em off you could say.'

'Kill them, you mean?' asked Don.

'Not necessarily,' said Bill, wriggling around in his seat rather uncomfortably. 'Anyways, once the goods were at the top of the cliff, that's where my great-great-grandfather came in, cuz 'ee, along with several others, would be waiting with pack ponies and carts, to take the goods to a safe inland 'ideaway, until arrangements could be made to get the goods where they needed to be, and…' he paused for effect, 'one of those 'ideaways was 'ere.'

'Here?' Several of us echoed together.

'Ah, I thought that 'ud surprise you all,' said Black Bill, delightedly. 'See, when the goods wuz brought back, they wuz stored in a secret room, which could only be reached by the smugglers' staircase. The room was secure enough, but if for any reason the customs men wuz tipped off and came into the pub, they'd 'ave to negotiate the smugglers' staircase before they stood any chance of seizing the goods, and catching those concerned.'

'What's a smugglers' staircase?' asked Don.

Black Bill leaned forward, clearly enjoying himself more and more as the story developed. 'The smugglers' staircase was a treacherous thing, for the treads wuz all shapes and sizes, different heights and different widths, making it almost impossible to climb in the dark, or even by candlelight, and making broken legs a certainty. This either ended the search immediately, or bought precious time for the smugglers.'

'How exciting,' I said. 'Does the staircase still exist?'

'I dare say it does,' said Black Bill. 'Although when I was a boy, the pub owners reckoned it had been boarded up for safety, even then.'

This wonderful story came to a timely end as Bod came over to join us during his obligatory visit to all the tables. As we all wished him happy birthday, his eyes turned to Mr Chan.

'Yin, you don't know how much it means that you've come here tonight,' he said.

'Ah, my friend, I always said that in times of trouble and strife I would be there for you, and I consider reaching your half century a troubling time.'

We all laughed, delighted by his gentle humour and watched, as he drew a small brown cardboard box out of his pocket, secured with a loop of cord that hooked over a tiny metal button.

'For you', he said, handing it to Bod.

Looking rather embarrassed, Bod opened the box, removed a piece of tissue paper and began to shake his head, obviously quite moved by what he saw.

'It's been many a long year since I've seen one of these,' he said.

'What is it, dear?' Asked Mrs Darley.

'A Moon Cake,' said Bod, handing the now open box to Mrs Darley.

We all leaned forward and peered eagerly into the little box which, much to my disappointment, simply housed a small, plain, round cake.

'Yin will explain,' said Bod, sitting down rather gingerly on the corner of the brass fender that surrounded the hearth, and so we settled once again for our second history lesson of the evening.

'The Moon cake is a token of my appreciation and

gratitude to Bod,' said Mr Chan, 'just as it is for Chinese people the world over who also eat Moon cakes as a token of thanks and remembrance.'

Don laughed. 'But why buy Bod a Moon Cake? What did he do to warrant such an honour?'

'He saved my life,' said Mr Chan simply.

The stunned silence was almost palpable.

'That was a long time ago, Yin. It doesn't matter now.'

'It matters to me, my friend,' said the Chinese man. 'It will always matter to me.'

There was a poignant silence, during which it became clear that the story of Bod saving Mr Chan's life was not about to be told. I knew Bod had served in the Navy for many years, and had to content myself with the fact that this must have happened during that time.

Mr Chan continued, 'It is most appropriate that we have spoken of smugglers and the Moon this evening, for my story too follows a similar theme, and will perhaps explain why the Moon cake is such a revered gift.

'To the ancient Chinese, unlike your smugglers, the Moon was a friend, as they planted, harvested, and worshipped by its phases. In fact, during the Tang Dynasty of the seventh to tenth centuries, it was considered so important, that it was given its own day of honour, and on the fifteenth day of the eighth Chinese month, the 'Moon festival' was celebrated, because it was deemed to be the brightest Moon of the year.'

'Is it still celebrated?' Asked Mrs Darley.

'It is indeed, my dear lady,' replied Mr Chan. 'The festival is celebrated by the Chinese people all over the world.

'You see, in the thirteenth and fourteenth centuries, China was ruled by the Mongols, who had overthrown the Sung dynasty in order to obtain power. The Chinese people at that time were suppressed.'

'In 1368 however, Lui Fu Tung of the Anhui Province, a loyal supporter of the Sung family, felt that enough was enough, and planned a rebellion. It was an almost impossible task, for how could he let everyone know where and when it was to take place?'

'No phones or postal system back then,' said Eddie.

'Indeed not,' Mr Chan smiled. 'However, it was during a moment of looking at the Moon one night, that the most wonderful idea came to Lui Fu Tung. Realising that the Moon festival was drawing near, he ordered the making of special cakes, saying that they were to commemorate the Moon festival and to bless the longevity of the Mongolian Emperor.'

'I take it that wasn't the real reason though?' Asked Phyllis shrewdly.

Mr Chan shook his head. 'No. The real purpose, was for the specially chosen bakers to smuggle a message into each cake, telling those to whom they were delivered, the details of the first rebellion and to be ready to 'Rise against the Tartars'.

'Eventually, this small, but successful uprising on the night of the Moon festival, when the full Moon smiled down upon them and lit their way, led to the Mongolian government eventually being overthrown. This, then, left the way clear for the beginning of the Ming dynasty.'

'How clever,' murmured Mrs Darley.

'And that my friends, is why the Chinese still eat Moon Cakes today - to be thankful and to remember. That is why, it seemed to me to be a most appropriate gift for the man who saved me from an early death.'

Bod said nothing, but simply rose to his feet and squeezed Mr Chan's shoulder in an act of thanks before moving on to see his other guests The rest of us meanwhile, were left in a state of subdued and wistful contemplation.

***

Walking down the path to the cottages some hours later, Mrs Darley looked up at the Moon and sighed.

'She is quite beautiful, isn't She?'

'Yes, She is,' I agreed.

'I think tonight has taught us all that the Moon can be a true friend to those who seek a worthy cause, and a fatal enemy to those who wish their deeds to be hidden.'

'A lady of contrasts,' I said.

Mrs Darley smiled. 'As all women should be my dear,' she said, turning her key in the lock.

I always feel sad for the waning Moon, as it hangs alone in the night sky, unappreciated by the majority as they sleep through Her visit. This led me to think of those who might still be awake to both greet and welcome Her quiet beauty, as She rises in the early hours, hence the title of this poem, 'Ladies of the Night'.

Ladies of the Night

When the final client has gone,
When the door is locked and bolted,
When the last lamp is extinguished,
Then, you come to me.

When my body is spent,
Sold to those seeking gratification,
You rise,
And I once again I belong to myself.

My mind is soothed,
My body eased,
My spirit made whole.

Stay with me now,
Through the pale light of dawn,
Release me not
Into the harsh light of day.

Here, I am unfettered,
Safe from the demands of men.
Here, beneath your diminishing light,
I am free.

Chapter Eleven

Dark Moon Magick

This is a time of ebony skies, when humankind is seemingly abandoned by the lady of the night, to flounder alone in the darkness. It is a time of dark deeds and clandestine meetings, and yet, through the darkness, comes our dreamtime and within the darkness, whispers of new life can be heard.

Some prefer not to practice magick at the dark Moon, as this phase is seen as a time when the Moon Goddess descends into the underworld and Her energy is at its lowest point. As such, this is often considered to be a period of inner reflection and stillness.

Others however, consider this an appropriate time to divine, using the divination tools to which they are drawn, be they runes, tarot, scrying, or the I-Ching, so that they might shine a light on the new month that is about to begin.

In our daily lives, the time of the dark Moon quite often brings a quiet period, where action is suspended in favour of rest and retrospection before the return of the light. This Moon phase is akin to the age of the Crone (or Elder for men), and the Goddess that reflects the duality of the dark Moon, is the Hindu Goddess Kali.

On a very superficial level, Kali is the Goddess often associated with sexuality, violence, and death. She is the terrifying shadow aspect of Parvati, the Goddess who embodies *Shakti*, the Hindu word to describe feminine energy, fertility, and creativity, and was said to have been created from Parvati's rage, when She was threatened by a demon called Rakta-bija. Once brought to life by Parvati's anger, Kali could neither be tamed, nor destroyed.

The enraged Kali unleashed her fury upon Rakta-bija, but as the demon lay bleeding, he began to multiply. Kali however, swept Her tongue across the battlefield, swallowing the multiplying demons, before finally sucking the life blood from the original Rakta-bija. These dual Goddesses are the wives of the Indian god Shiva, Lord of the Dance, and it is said that the dance of Kali will be the dance that ends the world.

Kali is depicted in many different ways, but is often seen as having two pairs of hands, two on the right side, and two on the left, three eyes, and a black or red tongue, which protrudes from Her dark face. Bloody human sacrifices were made to Kali in the hope that Her destructive tendencies would be pacified, and She is often seen feasting upon the flesh of Her victims, dancing upon their dismembered bodies, and wearing a necklace of their skulls.

Kali, however, is much maligned, for She is not merely the feared Crone Goddess, but is also the great Mother Goddess who is capable of teaching Her children harsh lessons, whilst also being fiercely protective of them. She is therefore not only the shadow side of Parvati, but like each of us, houses both darkness and light within Herself. This is illustrated perfectly by her two pairs of hands. The right-hand side symbolises Her as the great benefactor and Mother, sometimes carrying the Bowl of Life, or holding out Her hands in the *abhayamundra* pose, meaning 'fear not'. Her left hands meanwhile, depict Her as the destroyer, for here She holds a severed head and blood covered sword, with which to sever the thread of life.

Kali's destructive left hands can also symbolise the destruction of the ego – that which prevents us from being our authentic selves. Hence, to those who do not allow their ego to rule them, Kali can be the kind and benevolent Mother.

Although Kali is often misunderstood by many outside the Hindu religion, She nevertheless teaches valuable lessons to those willing to work on their spiritual self.

Kali lets us know in no uncertain terms, that death, like the dark Moon, is inevitable, as depicted by the hands on Her left- hand side that carry the sword, and the severed head. Rather than denying death however, Kali encourages us to accept and face it, albeit sometimes in the most terrifying of ways. The act of Kali dancing upon the bodies of the dead, symbolises the redundant nature of our outer shell once the soul has departed. We should not be appalled by Kali's actions, for once we have experienced physical death, Kali promises comfort, and eventual renewal as depicted by Her right-hand side, where She carries the Bowl of Life and adopts the *abhayamundra* pose.

This is why Kali is an important Goddess for those who are approaching the age of the Crone. She does not hide the inevitability that our bodies will fade in beauty and strength and that death will take us back to the Earth, but neither does She deny us knowledge of life's eternal cycle. Kali may beckon the Crone to her physical end, but always within Her bowl of life, the Maiden awaits.

Each dark Moon, Kali the destroyer calls us to let go of the twenty-eight-day cycle that has just passed, along with all its trials and challenges. She asks us to take advantage of the darkness, within which we might find peace and rest, before Her Mother aspect guides us back out into the light of a new lunar cycle.

A Dark Moon, Dark Mother Meditation

Sit quietly, somewhere you will not be disturbed. Play music, burn incense or oils of your choice (In keeping with the dual aspect of Kali, choose a combination of rich, dark oils, that remind us of our earthly connection, such as Vetivert or Myrrh, along with more spiritual oils which encourage inner reflection, and a connection with divinity, such as Frankincense and Sandalwood) and begin to become aware of your breathing, don't try to alter it in any way, but just become aware of its gentle rhythm, as you breathe in and out... in and out.

It is twilight and the season of winter is upon the land. You decide to leave the warmth of your cottage that sits of the edge of black marshland, and take advantage of the last remnants of light. As you step outside, you see a lone, naked tree standing on the horizon, its branches about to embrace the night that is to come, and you hear the unmistakable sound of geese flying back to their roosts before darkness settles.

A chill breeze stirs the rushes and you pull your cloak tightly around you, as you follow the path that skirts the marsh. Your feet crunch through fallen leaves and decaying bracken, whilst a creeping frost begins to harden the Earth, sparkling in the dying light.

As you continue your walk around the marsh, you suddenly become aware of the smell of burning wood, and in the distance, you can see tendrils of smoke curling up into the evening sky. Compelled to follow this evocative aroma, you become aware that you are walking towards the naked tree that you noticed from your cottage, and as the tree comes into view, you can just make out the flicker of a fire close to its base. You stand and watch for a moment as the orange flames seemingly dance around the trunk in the gathering darkness.

You decide to move nearer, and as you do so, you see the silhouette of a figure – a woman – tending a cauldron that hangs on a tripod above the fire. You watch, as she lifts the lid and sniffs the escaping steam. Edging closer you suddenly become aware of a rather pungent, earthy aroma filling the night air.

The unmistakable croak of a raven above your head makes you gasp as it takes flight from the top bough of the tree. As the woman turns to see what has startled the bird, she suddenly notices you, standing alone in the firelight.

You look at each other for a moment and you somehow feel drawn to her, despite her rather intimidating appearance, for this lady is tall and robed, with long grey hair that tumbles down her back. Around her neck are beads of bone and on a cord around her waist she wears a long pair of shears. Her eyes are dark, yet flecked, so you fancy, with silver.

The woman turns away from you and once more takes the lid from the cauldron. The earthy aroma immediately escapes on a plume of steam and you watch, as she picks up a large spoon and begins to ladle out the contents of the cauldron into a wooden goblet. She beckons you to come closer, and as you do so, she offers the goblet to you.

You take it from her outstretched hand and she indicates that you take a drink. You instinctively know that somehow you can trust this woman, and putting the goblet to your lips, you take a sip. The hot liquid is unfamiliar, and you ask what it is.

She turns to answer you, and now her dark eyes flash unmistakably with silver. 'It is Mugwort,' she says, 'Artemisia – sacred herb of the Moon Goddess, and I am Her priestess, Guardian of the Unseen Realms and the Dark Moon.'

You look at her, unsure for a moment what to say, but the priestess, sensing your unease continues, 'Drink of Artemisia to offer you protection when travelling to the inner realms in order to discover where your true path lies. For this is dark Moon, a time to journey with no one and nothing, other than your soul.'

She indicates that you sit upon a soft moss-covered mound beside the fire, and says: 'Stay awhile sister, and be still. Stay a while, and listen to the yearnings of your heart.'

And so you sit beside the fire with the priestess of the dark Moon, and journey inward to listen – listen to the yearnings of your heart...

***

Having listened and allowed your heart to speak, you know that it will soon be time to return to the winter's evening, the mossy mound, the firelight and the priestess of the Moon. With this realisation, comes the familiar croak of the raven.

But rather than returning to the grassy mound, you suddenly become aware that you are being lifted high, high into the dark winter sky, flying with ease above the leaping flames, above the naked tree and above the wet marshland. The land spreads out beneath you, and you instinctively know that during this next cycle of the Moon you will see things from a different perspective and have the ability to rise above your problems, for this is dark Moon, the time to let your heart speak, and your soul soar.

Feeling suddenly lighter than you have done for some time, you feel yourself being gently lowered back to the Earth, and within an instant, you are once again sitting on the mossy mound, beside which only the glowing embers of the fire remain. You look around and are disappointed to note that the priestess is nowhere to be seen, but at your feet sits a scroll, tied with a black ribbon.

You untie the ribbon, and as the scroll unravels, two items fall upon the ground which you pick up before reading the accompanying message:

'To my soul traveller:
A sprig of Mugwort for your shoe
To smooth and ease life's journey,
A raven's feather for your hair
So that you may always fly free'

You smile as you take the scroll, the sprig of Mugwort and the feather and place them safely in your pocket, and as you look towards the east, you see that the first shards of dawn are beginning to spread across the sky. You take one last look at the dying fire, and offer a silent word of thanks to all that you have seen and experienced, before walking back towards the path that circles the marsh.

From here, you once again crunch your way across frost gilded ground until you arrive at your cottage door, where the unmistakable sound of geese flying overhead signals the dawn. You take one last look at the naked tree, its branches reaching up to welcome the new day and you know without doubt, you are ready to face the new Moon cycle that is to come.

Now, whenever you are ready, gradually bring your awareness back to the present and when the moment feels right, just open your eyes.

Dark Moon Superstitions and Folklore:

Some believe that when the Moon is about to change from one cycle to another, i.e. at the dark/new Moon, it is a liminal time, when anything can happen, including mystical occurrences, and healing miracles.

It has been claimed by some scholars that the following verse which includes the words, 'a certain season', in the King James, version of the Bible, John 5:4, refers to the time of the dark Moon.

'For an angel went down at a certain season into the pool, and troubled the water: whosoever then first after the troubling of the water stepped in was made whole of whatsoever disease he had.'

There is also a Scottish cave at Dunksey Castle, in Dumfries and Galloway that was documented as having a healing spring, as late as 1791. Here the infirm, children with rickets, and those who were considered bewitched, were brought from great distances, to bathe in the healing waters which poured from the hill at '*...the change of the Moon*'.

The dark Moon also lends itself to divination, due to it being a time when outward light is withdrawn and we are called to journey within, in order to gain insight. Interestingly, this practice stretches back hundreds of years as is evidenced from Roman writings.

When Julius Caesar enquired why Ariovistus, leader of the Suebi and other allied Germanic peoples, had not engaged in battle with him, he was told that amongst the Germanic tribes it was customary for their seers or oracles to divine before battle as to whether it would be an auspicious time for them to fight. On this particular occasion, they declared that it was not the will of heaven that Ariovistus should lead his men into battle before the Moon had changed from dark, to new.

Whether they ignored future advice we shall never know, but Ariovistus *was* finally defeated at the Battle of Vosges in 58BCE and driven back over the Rhine by Caesar.

It is said that if Christmas day falls on a dark Moon, then the following year will be an auspicious one.

Dark Moon Celebrations and Rituals

A Moon celebration, regardless of the phase, can be as simple, or as complex as you wish, depending on preference and/or experience.

If you are well versed in formal magickal practice and wish to cast a spell, then the casting of a circle, changing your consciousness, path working and both feeling and visualising the outcome, will most probably form part of your Moon ritual.

If however, you just wish to acknowledge a particular Moon phase, then simply light a candle, burn incense or oils, play music of your choice, and perhaps use some of the suggestions given below to formulate your own Moon celebration.

A Dark Moon Altar

You may wish to set up a small altar in your home or garden and incorporate any of the following as decoration, or use ideas of your own:

- Pour some water into a black cauldron, to symbolise the dark Moon.

- Light a black candle, to represent the dark Moon, and a silver or white candle, to remind us that She is always present, even if we are unable to see Her.
- A black or purple altar cloth.
- Deep purple or dark red flowers/plant.
- A scrying or black mirror.
- Black Obsidian or Tourmaline for protection, scrying, and insight.
- A statue or totem animal, to represent a dark Goddess of your choice – for example, Kali, Ceridwen, Lilleth etc.
- Some form of divination that will guide you through this liminal time, such as a Tarot deck, or Rune stones.

Honouring the dark Moon usually takes place either the day before, the day following, or the day of its dark phase. Despite the fact that you will not be able to see the Moon, you can still go outside and acknowledge Her presence.

In order to prepare yourself, you may wish to take a few moments in which to mediate on what the dark Moon means to you and how you might journey within to gain insight for the Moon phase that is to come, or you may wish to use the guided visualization given earlier in this chapter.

Dark Moon Magick

The dark Moon is all about being still, on reflecting on what has been, what remains, and what is to come. It is a time for divination, for healing and also protection, as the Goddess of the Skies leaves us to journey alone in the darkness.

What follows, is a generic spell of how to make a dark Moon protection talisman, to carry with you throughout the next cycle of the Moon and to keep you safe from negative influences.

Dark Moon Protection Talisman

You will need:

- A piece of black felt, or material (approx 10-12cm square)
- A length of black ribbon (25-30cm)
- A teaspoon of lavender flowers
- A piece of black Obsidian or Tourmaline
- Three black thorns or three Rowan berries

Please note:

If you find it difficult to source some of the above, you can always substitute a small tumble stone of clear quartz for the obsidian or tourmaline. The black thorns or rowan berries can be substituted for rose thorns, and the teaspoon of lavender flowers can be replaced by three drops of lavender oil. Remember, it is your intent that is the most important aspect of magickal practice.

If you are using a crystal of any kind, ensure that you cleanse it thoroughly before using it in your spell work, in order to clear it of any negative energies, as set out in the steps below:

Cleansing your crystal:

- Submerge the crystal in water, preferably in the sea, a river, or a stream, although a bowl of rainwater, or filtered tap water will suffice. Alternatively, you can bury it in the Earth for twenty-four hours, or pass it through sage smoke.

- Energise the stone by leaving it exposed to sunlight, or moonlight for a few hours, or place it out in a thunderstorm.
- Programme the stone before using it in your talisman. Simply take a moment to hold your crystal and visualise clearly what its purpose is to be, before also verbalising your intent aloud – i.e. protection for you / your home / car etc.

Making your Protective Talisman

- Take your piece of material, place the crystal of your choice in the centre, along with the black thorns and/or rowan berries and lavender.
- Gather the material up and wrap the ribbon around it, saying the following knot rhyme as you secure it with three knots.

>'My magic I weave
>With this knot of one,
>Keeping my talisman
>True, safe and strong.

With intent I tie
This tight knot of two,
To keep me from harm
In all that I do.

On this dark Moon night
As I weave and I wind,
With this knot of three
May protection be mine.'

- You may then either carry the talisman with you for the next cycle of the Moon, or place it in your car, or home if that is more appropriate.

- When the dark Moon comes around again, you can undo your talisman, scatter the plant material onto the earth with a word of thanks, cleanse your crystal and repeat the same spell again for the next Moon cycle.

Dark Moon Blessing

Blessed be the Dark Moon.
She, whose light is extinguished,
Whose gaze is lost,
Whose black cloak enfolds the night.
Lead me/us across the abyss
So that I/we might hear
The truth that lies within my/our heart(s)

Toasting the Dark Moon

You may wish to raise a toast to the dark Moon, to simply acknowledge Her presence, or to give thanks.

Red wine, port, or any dark juice such as elderberry, blackcurrant, cranberry, or cherry, are all appropriate drinks with which to honour the Dark Mother. You may also wish to partake of some food in order to ground yourself, especially if you have carried out a meditation, or other form of spell work. Cakes or breads made with beetroot, or dark chocolate are appropriate, or if you prefer a healthier option, choose dark fruits such as plums, raisins, blackberries etc.

The Dark Moon represents the hidden aspects of us all – the shadow that we often wish to deny, but without which we could not function. We each have beauty within, but equally we all carry a thread of ugliness, we each have patience and compassion, but we also carry frustration and anger. We are each light and dark, fast and slow, heavy and light, for without polarity how could we ever hope to know harmony?

Kali depicts beautifully this dual aspect that we try so hard to mask. She is the ultimate loving Mother, teaching Her children both harsh lessons and unconditional love.

Ultimately, Kali cuts the fragile thread of life that we all so desperately cling to, plunging us into the dark abyss. She asks us however, to let go of our fear, for just like the endless cycle of the Moon, the darkness in which we momentarily find ourselves merely heralds the birth of the light.

Mrs Darley Tale: The Void

So, here I was at the appointed hour, having left my work

colleagues in the pub some forty-five minutes earlier and fervently hoping I would be in time.

Friday evening brought a dense summer mist, which wrapped itself around the cottages, and made me feel as though I was standing on the edge of the world. I stood on Mrs Darley's doorstep, shivering a little both from the damp air and the thought of what lay ahead.

As was often the case, I had received a passing invitation a few days previously to join Mrs Darley and guests for a 'Moon phase' celebration, together with a rather odd request saying that I should arrive around 8pm and to be prepared for 'the unusual', but that I was feel free to leave at any time if I felt uncomfortable.

'Come in, dear.' Mrs Darley greeted me on the doorstep and embraced me in a warm hug, before thrusting me into the midst of familiar, friendly faces that were bathed in the light from many candles and a roaring fire.

I briefly said hello to the other guests, who included Phyllis, Peter, Bod and Rose, as I sensed that Mrs Darley was anxious for proceedings to begin.

'Now, my dears,' she said, 'we must waste no time, for soon the Moon will set and our ritual must be done before She leaves our skies. The rug, dear...' Mrs Darley signalled to Bod, who promptly rolled up her beautiful Persian rug and placed it carefully behind the settee.

My eyes were immediately drawn to a five-pointed star carved into the now exposed black slate floor, and I felt my heart begin to thud with anxiety, for wasn't this star the sign of the dark arts - of the Devil? I fleetingly recalled the words of Oscar Wilde as he described fear, *'It is as if one's heart were beating itself to death in some empty hollow'*.

Feeling totally alone in my own empty hollow, I was momentarily distracted by Peter, who placed a small coffee table, covered with a white cloth, on the centre of the star, upon which he set two large pillar candles and a small, silver bell.

Bod and Mrs Darley then made a brief foray into the kitchen, returning moments later with a variety of items. Bod was carrying a large bundle of hazel sticks, a few pairs of pliers and some twine, which he placed in front of the coffee table, whilst Mrs Darley followed closely behind, bearing a wicker basket, and a large carrier bag that she placed beneath the table.

'I think that's everything', she said, 'so if everyone is ready, we really ought to make a start.'

Immediately, the others began to form a circle around the perimeter of the star, and I finally found myself sandwiched between Phyllis and Bod.

Mrs Darley then rang the bell, a beautiful clear note, which not only lingered in the air, but also exerted a calming effect upon my thudding heart and racing mind.

She raised her left hand in the air. 'It has begun.'

She proceeded to light an incense stick from the candle on the table, placing it in a wooden holder and carrying it clockwise around the outside of our circle. As she did so, she said, 'With the sweet breath of air, and the heat of fire, I purify and cleanse our sacred space.'

She then replaced the incense holder back on the table, before lifting a small bowl of water, into which she sprinkled what looked like salt. Once again, she moved in a clockwise direction around the outside of our circle, sprinkling the liquid as she walked, whilst saying, 'With the Water of life and the salt of the Earth, I purify and cleanse our sacred space.'

She then replaced the dish on the table, and assumed her place in the circle once more. Turning to her left, she took Rose's right hand in hers and said, 'As my hand joins yours, our sacred space is cast.'

Rose smiled at her, then turned to *her* left and, taking Peter's right hand in hers, she announced, 'As my hand joins yours, our sacred space is cast.'

The same actions were repeated around the circle, until it was time for me to take Bod's hand in mine, and repeat the words the others had used. I could feel my heart thudding once again as all eyes turned towards me. Much to my surprise however, the words flowed easily and it felt surprisingly empowering to speak them aloud.

'As my hand joins yours, our sacred space is cast.'

With the circle finally complete, there was a momentary silence, before Mrs Darley said, very calmly and precisely, 'Our circle is cast. We stand between the realms of Earth and of Spirit.'

I stood with a feeling of both wonder and disbelief at having taken part in such a strange ritual. Part of me felt at peace, yet another part was anxious about what would – or could – follow. Looking around however, at the friendly and familiar faces illuminated by candlelight and fire glow, I thought they had never looked so alive, yet so serene, and gradually all thoughts of dark acts vanished from my mind.

Mrs Darley then stepped into the centre of the circle and bade us all sit on the small silk cushions, which she handed out from the carrier bag beneath the table.

'Tonight, my dears, our ritual is to be kept simple, as is our work, for this is one of those rare occasions when the black Moon visits our skies, and the black Moon,' she said, turning to me, 'is when we acknowledge the birth of a second new Moon in any calendar month.'

I smiled and nodded my understanding.

'The black Moon is a time at which our thoughts must turn to protection, for the Black Lady is a bewitching and beguiling creature. She is the Enchantress who has often tempted mankind beyond their capabilities, beyond their marriage beds and certainly beyond their better judgment.'

Gentle laughter rippled around the circle before she continued. 'So, tonight we will make our protective pentagrams before the black Moon sets. I am sure most of you are familiar with the symbolic aspect of the pentagram, but for those of you who are not, let me explain.'

I listened carefully, hoping her explanation would dispel my confusion, for although I was convinced that the sign of the pentagram was used to depict evil practices (if the films I had seen were anything to go by), hadn't Mrs Darley just used the word 'protective'?

'The pentagram,' she said, 'is one of the most misunderstood symbols of our time. It is often hailed as the symbol of the devil by the Christian Church, and is almost always used in films depicting black magick, or satanic rites.

'The simple truth is, that it is one of the oldest symbols known to man, and has been used in protection rites for millennia. To some it represents the elements of Air, Fire, Water, Earth and Spirit, whilst to others it represents mankind himself, as portrayed in Leonardo's Vetruvian Man.'

A simple pentagram made from five hazel twigs

I stared at the pentagram carved into the floor, and suddenly began to see it in a different light.

'Another explanation, and one that I personally favour,' she continued, 'was suggested by a lady whose work some of you will be familiar with - Doreen Valiente.'

There was a murmur of recognition within the circle, and although I remembered Mrs Darley mentioning Doreen Valiente as the author of the beautiful words which she called 'The Charge', several months earlier, I still knew very little about her.

'Doreen,' continued Mrs Darley, 'suggests that the top point of the star represents the source, the light, the Godhead, the Goddess, or whatever you care to call it. The lower right-hand point represents the descent of humankind from the Source to Earth, whilst the middle, left-hand point, represents our climb in consciousness in order to accumulate a certain amount of spiritual knowledge. The middle, right-hand point, represents our knowledge plateauing out, whilst the lower, left-hand point, represents our fall into the abyss and subsequent loss of spiritual connection. We are now faced with the final long haul back to the top of the pentagram or the Source, whilst attempting to recapture all that has been lost.'

I sat in silence, attempting to process this latest piece of information, but Mrs Darley, who was anxious to proceed, urged, 'Come then my dears, let us begin our craft work.'

Phyllis must have noticed the look of confusion on my face, because she whispered gently, 'You'll need five sticks and five bits of twine, then just do what I do.'

I nodded, and following her lead, I successfully created my very first pentagram, proudly setting it on the floor in front of me, just as everyone else had done. With all the pentagrams complete, Mrs Darley once again stepped into the circle, and rang her bell.

'May these sacred pentagrams serve us well, to protect our homes, our loved ones, our judgment, and if needs be, help protect us from ourselves.'

We all laughed, but I have little doubt that we realised the truth of her words, for very often it is our own actions that cause us all the most unrest. At this point, the wicker basket was brought out from beneath the table which contained a feast of delicious food. Small pasties, fresh bread and an abundance of cheese and fruit, all nestled cosily next to five glasses, and two bottles of rich, dark, wine.

With the food shared and the wine poured, Mrs Darley stood and raised her glass, 'May these pentagram talismans bring us all protection, as the Black Lady, twice born Moon Goddess of the summer skies, looks down upon our world. To protection, and the Black Lady.'

'To protection, and the Black Lady,' we echoed.

We then unwound our circle and having enjoyed a further hour of socialising, I eventually found myself standing on Mrs Darley's doorstep, clutching my pentagram and expressing my thanks for an unexpectedly enlightening evening.

'I'm glad you enjoyed it my dear,' she said, 'although I couldn't help but notice the look on your face when the rug was rolled back and you saw the pentagram on the floor.'

I laughed nervously, feeling slightly embarrassed by my initial thoughts of black magick and devil worship.

'What did you imagine was going to happen?' she asked gently.

'I'm not really sure. Something... dark perhaps?'

She smiled, 'Ah, so that was the problem – fear of the unknown. Fear is a natural and necessary emotion, it keeps us safe from harm, but by the same token it can be debilitating, paralysing and often prevents us from living life to the full. Sometimes, just as you did tonight, you must close your eyes and jump into the void, and very often, my dear,' she added with a smile, 'the results are priceless.'

This poem was written following Mrs Darley's warnings about the Black Moon being a time of deception and illusion. We must therefore, try not to become deceived by something, simply because it may look beautiful and innocent.

The Black Lady

The Black Lady calls,
Her beauty deceives,
Trust not in the words
She would have you believe
That everything is,
Simply as you perceive,
Beware, beware the Black Lady.

The Black Lady calls,
Her innocence belies,
A sinister presence
Beneath the disguise,
My child, listen not
To her dark web of lies,
Beware, beware the Black Lady.

Beware the Black Lady,
She who calls twice,
Be charmed by her beauty
But aware of her price,
For the black Moon will bind you,
Enchant and entice,
Beware, beware the Black Lady.

Chapter Twelve

Moon Set

Mrs Darley Tale: Jalani

'Here we are,' I said, as I walked into Mrs Darley's bedroom, carrying a tray holding three glasses of iced mint tea, and a plate of cherry shortbreads. 'Hopefully this will cheer everyone up.'

'Mmm,' murmured Lucy, eyeing the shortbreads as I set down the tray on the bedside table. She was perched on the end of Mrs Darley's bed, having just finished reading to her from a rather dog-eared book.

'That's very kind of you my dear,' said Mrs Darley, struggling to sit up before taking her glass of iced tea.

'Are you feeling any better?' I asked, as I walked around the bed to help rearrange her pillows. I wasn't used to seeing my neighbour so unwell.

'I'm improving as each minute passes,' she smiled weakly. 'Fortunately, these migraines don't happen very often, but when they do, they come in clusters, and I have little choice but to take to my bed.'

'I can't imagine what they must be like,' I said. 'I sometimes suffer from tension headaches and they're bad enough, but at least they don't literally knock me off my feet.'

'Well hopefully this will soon ease,' said Mrs Darley. 'I just feel sorry that it's happened today, when Lucy is staying.'

'Have your Mum and Dad gone somewhere nice?' I

asked, handing a glass of iced tea to Lucy.

'Out for dinner I think,' she said, turning her attention to the cherry shortbreads, which were obviously of far more interest than her parents' current whereabouts.

'It's their wedding anniversary,' explained Mrs Darley, 'so I said that Lucy could stay here for the night, and then Rose and Bod wouldn't have to hurry back, but of course I hadn't bargained for having a migraine.'

'We'll soon get you better,' said Lucy kindly, attempting to dunk her shortbread rather unsuccessfully into her glass of iced tea.

'How could I fail to feel better with you two lovely ladies looking after me?' Mrs Darley smiled, taking few sips of her drink. 'I have one of you to bring me tea and biscuits and the other to read me a story.'

'We've finished the story now though,' said Lucy. She gazed wistfully at the book she had just placed down on the bed.

'What was it about?' I asked.

'Oh, thieves and heroes and treasure hunters. It was really exciting.'

'It's an old book of my daughter's actually,' said Mrs Darley, called *Rye Royal*, by Malcolm Saville, but it's still a great adventure, even though it's a bit old fashioned now in many ways.'

Lucy sighed, 'I wish we had another story to read though.' She turned to me. 'Do you know any, Carole?'

I shook my head, 'No, not really.'

'You could make one up,' she said, hopefully.

'Oh Lucy,' said Mrs Darley, 'perhaps Carole's had a busy day and is too tired to make up stories.'

I felt sorry for Lucy. She had been so good, reading to Mrs Darley, and never once complained that she hadn't been able to go out to do any of the things they'd had planned for the day.

'Well,' I said, 'I do have a story I wrote for a competition some time ago, but never thought it was good enough to enter. I can go and get that if you like?'

Lucy clapped her hands in delight. 'Oh yes. What's it about?'

'A boy and the Moon,'

'Perfect,' said Mrs Darley with a contented sigh, as she settled back against her pillows. 'We'll both be ready and waiting.'

Within five minutes, I returned to the warmth of Mrs Darley's bedroom, along with a few sheets of rather tattered paper covered in my untidy handwriting. I kicked off my shoes, perched alongside Lucy on the edge of Mrs Darley's bed and began to read my story…

Homes were flooded, rivers burst their banks, mud slides blocked railway tracks, farmers' fields were saturated, but still the rains came. On and on, relentless and unforgiving. It brought a variety of responses from Jalani's neighbours, who had lived in these extreme conditions for what seemed like an eternity.

'I must buy a new umbrella.'

'I must put more sandbags across my door,'

'I must arrange an indoor venue for my birthday party.'

'I wish I hadn't bothered booking that holiday.'

'I haven't got any use out of that new barbeque.'

Most people saw the rain merely as an inconvenience, something to escape from, something to scowl at, something that made them feel very ungrateful. Not one stopped for a moment in their busy and often futile lives to ask, 'why is this happening?'

They had discussed the rain in school. The general consensus of opinion, as Jalani knew and accepted, was climate change - global warming, caused by mankind's impact upon his environment. Wednesday afternoons had now been dedicated to a new school project called, 'Climate Change Awareness'.

'Of course,' said Mrs Matthews, the geography teacher, who had been appointed to run the project, 'in times past, man would have seen freak weather patterns like this as proof that the gods were displeased, and they would make sacrifices to placate them.'

The classroom filled with laughter.

'Naturally, we don't need to deal in superstition anymore,' said Mrs Matthews, flushed with pleasure because her quip about the gods had resulted in such hilarity. 'We have science.'

Jalani looked out of the classroom window, and looked up at the slated clouds scurrying across the sky. He suddenly felt desperately sorry for this apparently civilized environment in which he found himself, with its curiously limited view of the world and its wonders. He did of course, appreciate the discoveries of science, but he came from a place where other wonders were of equal importance.

His homeland may have been poor, it may not have had the technological wonders of the west and the advances of medical science, but what it did have, was a connection to the natural world, Her moods, Her voice, and Her medicines.

'Always listen, Jalani,' his Grand-mother had whispered as she took his hand in hers the last time he had visited. 'Listen to the Earth and to the Moon, for they alone speak the language of the universe. The Earth is our home – our Mother - and the Moon is our ruler, governing tides and time, the atmosphere and the weather.'

Seven-year-old Jalani had sat and watched as his Grand-mother appeared to fall asleep. He was unsure what she meant as she lay there on her make-shift bed, covered only by a multi-coloured blanket, but he had smiled at her, and promised he would always listen.

Moments later, she opened her eyes and tightened her grip upon his hand. 'And always remember, Jalani,' she said, 'remember that whenever you ask the universe for anything, there must be an exchange of energy. You must give in order to receive. It is the law.'

'I will remember, Grandma,' he whispered.

She smiled at him. 'I have no regrets, Jalani, that my son took you *to the modern world, for your life will, in many ways be easier, but in others, it will be so much harder. The voice of the Great Mother will be silenced, for there they have other gods – manmade gods.'*

And now, eight years later, he heard again the words of his Grandmother and knew what he must do.

***

Upon returning home later that afternoon, Jalani ran upstairs to his room and opened the drawer in his bedside table. He pulled out a small red velvet bag, secured with a leather cord, and tucked it safely into the front of his rucksack, along with his torch, which always lay beneath his bed in case of emergencies. Leaning across his bed, he picked up a small Moonstone crystal from his window ledge and placed it in the back pocket of his jeans. He then ran quickly down the stairs, grabbed his coat and headed for the front door.

'Where are you going Jalani? Dinner's almost ready.' Jalani could hear the frustration in his mother's voice.

'I won't be long.'

'But it's getting dark and it's still pouring with rain…Jalani… Jalani…'

Jalani knew that on this occasion he must close his ears to his mother's pleas, and slamming the door behind him, ran down the hill towards the river, his face being lashed unmercifully by the rain.

The metal signs were still there, in the middle of the road.

'DANGER. RIVER IN FLOOD. BRIDGE CLOSED'

Jalani glanced over his shoulder to ensure he was alone, before edging his way around the sign, and venturing onto the bridge. Gingerly, he made his way to the centre of the bridge, where, for the first time, he felt afraid. Here, the roar of the water was almost deafening, and he could feel its vibration as it thundered against the underside of the bridge only inches below his feet.

For a brief moment he thought about his classmates, Mrs Matthews the geography teacher and especially his parents. They would all think him mad. The authorities had closed the bridge for fear of collapse, and now here he was, standing in the middle of it, alone, in the gathering darkness, with no one knowing where he was. For a moment he questioned the sanity of his actions, but then, if he didn't do it, no one else would. They weren't to blame - it was just the way it was. Society had taught them different values.

Jalani however, had listened to his Grand-mother's words, and to the language of Earth and Moon. He understood that the Earth was saturated and unable to bring forth the harvest that was so desperately needed, and that in order for this to happen, the Moon must refrain from shedding her tears via the atmospheric conditions she had created and he was the one who had to ask...

In his heart and mind, he heard his Grand-mother's voice. *'Whenever you ask the universe for anything, there must be an exchange of energy. You must give in order to receive. It is the law.'*

This was the purpose of sacrifice - to make an act sacred.

Jalani slipped the rucksack off his back and quickly unzipped it, immediately taking out his torch and switching it on, before fumbling around for the little velvet bag. Once in his possession, he loosened the drawstring and allowed a selection of small stones and pebbles to fall upon the wet tarmac.

Jalani, began to work quickly, for the rush of the river grew suddenly much louder, and the bridge groaned with a mixture of fear and displeasure, almost as if it knew of its impending fate. The rain was relentless, pounding on his back, as though it was trying to hammer him into the ground.

Within minutes, the pebbles had been fashioned into two small mounds which sat adjacent to one another, and Jalani sat back on his heels to inspect his work. Then, taking the small round moonstone crystal from the back pocket of his jeans, he leaned forward and placed it between the two mounds. He scrambled to his feet, turned his face to the heavenly deluge and raising his arms, shouted loud above the roaring waters.

'Lady Moon, come back to us. Shine again in the night sky. I know the tears you shed are because you think we have forgotten you, forgotten that without you our world as we know it would not exist. We have become distracted by material wonders, and have forgotten how to show you gratitude. We have forgotten how to sing to you, how to dance in your honour, how to search for your face between the hills, but some of us do remember. My Grand-mother taught me to remember.' He indicated the two mounds of pebbles that he had built, with the moonstone standing between them.

'This is my Moon temple, which I dedicate to you and in return, I ask that you come back and light our night skies once again.'

Jalani sank down beside the mound of pebbles, his energy spent, as the rains continued to lash against his face, and saturate every piece of his clothing.

He suddenly became aware that not only was the thundering vibration of the water increasing, but the bridge was creaking, almost as though its pain was too much to bear. Suddenly the support on the far side of the bridge gave way, and the tarmac above was greedily consumed by the black roaring waters.

Jalani scrambled to his feet, his heart pounding as hard and fast as the rain was falling. He picked up his rucksack and almost flew back across the bridge, running, running, running, until he felt safe enough to stop.

Eventually, exhausted, he collapsed onto a saturated grassy bank, and watched in disbelief as the bridge upon which he had made his offering to the Moon, had now fallen, claimed and carried away on the furious torrent, towards the open mouth of the sea.

In that moment, he understood that his life could so easily have been sacrificed there on that bridge, but instead, his gift of the Moon temple had been taken. It alone had been enough.

Shaking, with his heart slamming against his ribs, Jalani stood up, his feet sliding on the sodden grass and as he did so, he suddenly *became aware that the rain no longer drummed out its relentless rhythm upon his head. The Earth had fallen silent. The clouds had parted. The Moon had dried Her tears.*

'And I might just have to dry my tears,' Mrs Darley said, gently patting my hand and looking up at me from her pale blue pillow.

'I didn't mean to make you cry,' I said, 'especially on top of everything else.'

'Oh, this migraine is just a blip, but your story was just the tonic I needed.'

'Well, I'm glad you liked it,' I said.

'It was lovely, and it stirred the emotions, like all good stories should.' She turned to Lucy. 'Did you enjoy it?'

'Yes,' sighed Lucy, 'and I'm in love with Jalani.'

'Ah,' said Mrs Darley, 'we ladies often find the combination of a hero and a compassionate soul quite irresistible.'

'Do you have any other stories?' Lucy asked.

'Not tonight she doesn't,' said Mrs Darley. 'I promised your mother you would be in bed before nine o clock.'

'She won't know if you don't tell her.'

'Maybe not, Lucy dear, but *I* will know. Anyway, it's already quarter past nine, and we've kept Carole here long enough, so say goodnight now, and go and make yourself comfortable in the bedroom next door.'

With Lucy gone, I drew Mrs Darley's curtains, switched on the lamp, and ensured she had fresh water.

'I'll check on Lucy in a minute,' I said, 'but is there anything else I can do for you before I go?'

'Yes, my dear, there is.'

I looked at her expectantly.

'Never stop telling stories,' she said.

The Setting of the Moon

The journey from Moon rise to Moon set, is one that can be made over and over again as time evaporates into infinity, for life is a cyclic dance, and when we take time to ebb and flow in rhythm with the lunar phases, we hold the key to transforming our lives.

Each new born crescent offers us the opportunity to sow seeds, every waxing Moon gives us the impetus to move ahead, each full orb helps us bring our projects to completion, every waning Moon provides a chance to enjoy the fruits of our labours and each dark Moon encourages us to rest, reflect and dream once again in the darkness.

Our beautiful nocturnal visitor changes the thoughts and feelings of everyone who falls beneath Her gaze. She invites us to dream beyond all measure and to love without limits, but bids us also remember that She is the Lady of Contrasts, the one who calls us to explore our shadow side and flirt with temptation.

William Butler Yeats, the Irish poet, captures the effects of the Moon perfectly in this quote from his essay entitled, *The Symbolism of Poetry*, written in 1900.

'If I look at the moon herself and remember any of her ancient names and meanings, I move among divine people, and things that have shaken off our mortality, the tower of ivory, the queen of waters, the shining stag, among enchanted woods, the white hare sitting upon the hilltop, the fool of faery with his shining cup full of dreams....'

The Moon sees into the very core of our being and from Her, nothing is hidden. She is the keeper of a thousand secrets and beneath Her, we discover our true selves.

Mrs Darley Tale: Midnight Magick

The sound of an owl disturbed my sleep, and I awoke to the light of the full Moon shining through the bedroom window, lending an almost opalescent quality to the room.

Feeling restless, I threw back the covers and walked over to the window, lifting my eyes to the full-bodied Moon. She was beautiful, but more than that, She was radiant, almost as though She had seen something which warmed Her heart.

She held my gaze until I suddenly became distracted by a glimmer of light in the far corner of the field adjacent to the cottage gardens. I allowed my eyes to wander - there it was again, flashes of intermittent orange.

I stood, fascinated, straining my eyes to try and make out the source of the mysterious lights. Eventually, unable to satisfy my curiosity and perhaps just a little bewitched by the light of the Moon, I pulled on my jeans, threw a shirt around my shoulders and made my way out onto the path which led down to the old pigsties at the top of the field. The night was warm and seemed to pulsate with the energies flowing from the Moon.

From here, I began to skirt my way along the northern perimeter of the field, until the overhanging hedge, which offered me some protection, began to peter out. I stopped and looked. The vision before me made my heart quicken, for I could now see that the orange light was a fire, and the intermittent flashes were actually caused by the silhouettes of people dancing in a circle around it.

I longed to move closer and decided to edge my way along to the next obvious area of shelter beneath the thorn, just a few yards distant. There, I sank down thankfully onto the dewy grass, and as I did so, I became aware of voices - beautiful harmonious voices.

Entranced, I watched, as the singing and dancing stopped and a bare breasted woman stepped forward to kneel before what appeared to be a round flat stone, from which she took two goblets. Rising to her feet and turning her back towards me, she raised the goblets to the sky as if toasting the Moon before uttering words which were sadly lost to me on the night air.

Totally entranced by the scene playing out before me, I was suddenly startled by a rustling sound to my right, and was surprised to see a small fox appear through a gap in the dry-stone wall. Within an instant he headed off across the field, and being afraid that he would draw attention to my hiding place, I chose my moment and hurried to the shelter of the hedge, before quickly making my way back to my cottage.

Once ensconced in the safety of my bedroom, I was disappointed to note that the Moon was no longer visible and the room had darkened. I immediately looked across to the far corner of the field, but could see no trace of the fire that had so captured my imagination.

I reluctantly returned to the warmth and comfort of my bed, and was just becoming seduced into that blissful state between reality and sleep, when I momentarily became aware of footsteps on the gravel path outside my window, followed by the unmistakable tinkle of Mrs Darley's wind chimes…

***

When morning came, the sun beckoned me into the garden and I stood in the middle of the lawn, entranced by the vibrant colour and perfumed beauty of midsummer.

'Hello dear,' the familiar voice of Mrs Darley called to me from her cottage door. 'A charming morning.'

I turned and smiled, 'My thoughts exactly.'

'The beauty of the Earth is enhanced by the fact that both the Sun and the Moon are at the height of their power, and it is inevitable that we too fall under their spell,' she said, waving her hand towards the heavens.

'In what way?' I asked, looking up, and sheltering my eyes with my hand against the glare of the Sun.

'Well, the midsummer Sun calls us to adventure and distant horizons, whilst the Blessing Moon tempts us from our slumber and bids us walk through an enchanted dreamscape, where only we can decide between what is real and what we may only have imagined.'

This rather strange statement was left hanging in the air, almost as if she knew, as if she'd seen…

'What do you mean by "what we may only have imagined…?"' I began, turning to face her.

But, just as the dark Moon slips away from the night sky, so Mrs Darley too, had already slipped from view.

This poem was written after looking up at the Moon, and wondering whether She yearns for the days when She was acknowledged by all as the Queen of Heaven. In our modern world, Her popularity has been overshadowed by artificial lights and virtual worlds but - just occasionally - when Her full light falls upon the Earth, I hope Her heart is warmed by those who remember Her still.

Still

Once,
Once, long ago
When the Earth was young,
My name was Diana,
Queen of Heaven.

The sun would defer to me,
Stars would bow down to me,
And mankind would worship me.

But now,
Now, the Earth is old,
They have forgotten my name.

Sometimes,
Sometimes when the night is still
And the ocean reflects the heavens,
I look down into mirrored waters
And wonder.
I wonder why I am not loved.

My pale light still shines in the darkness,
The earth I continue to gild in liquid silver,
And my face -
My face retains still its youthful beauty.

And yet,
No longer does a watcher wait for me,
No longer is a temple built for me,
No longer do lovers swear upon me.

I hang,
Suspended,
Forgotten.
Curtains are drawn against my face.
Street lamps glare - outshine my light.

But sometimes,
Sometimes when my face is full
I gaze down upon the Earth,
And I see them.

Around flame and fire
They dance,
Willing my energy to meld with theirs.

And, in that moment I know,
I am still young,
I am still beautiful,
I am still loved.

ABOUT THE AUTHOR

Carole Carlton is a writer, speaker and workshop facilitator in many aspects of Pagan practice and complementary health. She is a Reiki Master / Teacher with the UK Reiki Federation and owns 'Mrs Darley's Herbal', a herbal and Pagan giftware shop in Worcestershire, which is also online at:
www.arcanus.co.uk/shop

Carole spends her time between the forests of Middle England and the wild landscape of her beloved Cornwall, sharing both with her husband, William and tiny Jack Russell, Pippin.

She can be contacted in the following ways:

Via her website
www.arcanus.co.uk

Via Facebook
www.facebook.com/profile.php?id=100003282347984

Via Instagram
@mrsdarley

Books in the Mrs Darley Series:

Mrs Darley's Pagan Whispers
Mrs Darley's Moon Mysteries
Mrs Darley's Pagan Elements
Mrs Darley's Pagan Healing Wisdom
Mrs Darley's Pagan Paths to Magick
Mrs Darley's Practical Pagan Magick
Mrs Darley's Fragrant Herbal

Printed in Great Britain
by Amazon